Adobe® PHOTOSHOP® 7

ONE-CLICK WOW!

Jack Davis & Linnea Dayton

Adobe

Adobe Photoshop 7 One-Click Wow!

Jack Davis and Linnea Dayton

Peachpit Press
1249 Eighth Street
Berkeley, CA 94710
(510) 524-2178
(510) 524-2221 (fax)

Find us on the World Wide Web at:
http://www.peachpit.com/wow

Peachpit Press is a division of Pearson Education
Adobe Photoshop 7 One-Click Wow! is published in association with Adobe Press

To report errors, please send a note to errata@peachpit.com

Copyright © 2003 by Jack Davis and Linnea Dayton
Cover design: Jack Davis
Book design: Jill Davis
Production and prepress: Jonathan Parker
Direct-to-plate printing: Quebecor World / Taunton, Massachusetts

Notice of Liability:
The information in this book and the software on the CD-ROM that accompanies the book are
distributed on an "as is" basis, without warranty. While every precaution has been taken in the
preparation of this book, neither the authors nor Peachpit Press shall have any liability to any
person or entity with respect to any liability, loss, or damage caused or alleged to be caused directly
or indirectly by the instructions contained in this book or by the computer software and hardware
products described herein or provided on the CD-ROM that accompanies the book.

ISBN 0-321-12531-2

0 9 8 7 6 5 4 3 2 1

Printed and bound in the United States of America

To the National Association of Photoshop Professionals (NAPP) and KW Training (the "outreach" associate of NAPP) for doing more than any other organization to "evangelize" the worldwide creative community about the incredible capabilities of our beloved Photoshop. And to the fearless (and demented) leader of both of the above, Scott Kelby. The man is on a mission to change the world, and I'm always inspired by his passion to do so.

— Jack Davis

To Heifer International for so effectively addressing challenges that can't be met with just one click. A portion of the royalties from this book will be donated to this exemplary humanitarian-aid project (www.heifer.org).

— Linnea Dayton

ACKNOWLEDGMENTS

We had a great deal of help in putting this book and CD-ROM together. First, we appreciate the support of Christopher Sluka from Olympus for providing Jack with their Camedia E-20 SLR digital camera, which he used to take many of the photos in the book. We also want to thank the friends and family who let us "style" some of their photos to help illustrate the pages. And our thanks go to Piper Carr and others at Corbis Images who allowed us to use photos from their Royalty Free collections.

Several people helped make sure this CD-and-book package communicates clearly: We are especially grateful to Jill Davis for designing the book; to Garen Checkley for beta-testing and copy-editing; to Cher Threinen-Pendarvis for beta-testing and proofreading; to Jonathan Parker for managing production, producing the pages, and preparing them for printing.

We'd also like to thank the many supporters at Peachpit Press — in particular, our editor Cary Norsworthy, Adobe Press editor Kelly Ryer, publisher Nancy Ruenzel, production coordinator Kate Reber, and technical-expert-supreme Victor Gavenda, who beta-tested and engineered the CD-ROM.

Finally, thanks to all who have helped us with eight editions of *The Photoshop Wow! Book*. The experience we gained in that project has made *Adobe Photoshop 7 One-Click Wow!* possible, and we're delighted to pass it on.

CONTENTS

HOW TO USE THIS BOOK & CD-ROM

The book tells how to apply and customize the hundreds of One-Click Wow! Presets on the CD-ROM.

▶ *Throughout the book are tips in this format — starting with an orange pointer to catch your eye. The tips provide useful information about working with the One-Click Wow Presets in Photoshop 7. Here are some tips you may find especially useful:*

- *Converting a Background to a layer that can accept Styles (page 4)*
- *Understanding the relationship between the **One-Click Wow! Styles** and your file's Resolution setting (page 10)*
- *Controlling brush tip size with keyboard shortcuts (page 80)*
- *Using Photoshop 7's new Healing Brush (page 86)*
- *Choosing a file format for saving your finished image (page 20)*

Here's what you'll find on the *Adobe Photoshop 7 One-Click Wow!* CD-ROM:

- **More than 300 sophisticated Layer Styles** for enhancing your photos, type, and artwork (in the **Wow 7-Styles** folder)
- **Another 150 Styles, especially for buttons,** plus **50 combined Rollover Styles** for automatic interactivity (in the **Wow 7-20 Button Styles.asl** file, also in the **Wow 7-Styles** folder)
- **Wow-Styles Tutorial.psd files** for practicing all aspects of working with Styles (in the **Wow-Styles Tutorial** folder)
- **Wow Tool Presets** that imitate traditional art media such as watercolor, oils, and chalk. Some of these Presets are designed for "cloning" a source image as a painting using Photoshop's **Pattern Stamp** and **Art History Brush** tools. Others are designed for painting from scratch with the **Brush** tool.

*Here the **Wow 7-AH Watercolor** (left) and the **Wow 7-AH Chalk** (right) produce very convincing and quite different results in cloning a photo of an apple as a painting.*

- Other **Wow Tool Presets,** for tasks such as cropping and improving photos. Besides **Wow-Crop** and **Marquee** Presets, you'll find **Wow-Image Fix Presets** for using the Brush tool to lighten and darken specific areas of an image, to correct "red-eye," to whiten teeth and eyes, and to neutralize redness on the skin. (All of the Wow Tool Presets are in the **Wow 7-Tools** folder.)

- **More than 60 Wow Actions** (in the **Wow 7-Photoshop Actions** folder) that give you quick, automated options for creating special effects and carrying out production tasks. A few of the complex dimensional effects you'll find for type and graphics are brushed metal, crystal, and fire. Effects for photos include soft focus, blurred background, watercolor, line work, stippling, mezzotint, bordering, and colorizing. Automated production tasks include tone and color corrections and others. Try them out on the files in the **Wow-Actions Testers** folder.

With the Actions palette in Button Mode, the Wow Actions appear in color-coded sets.

- **40 Gradient Presets** (in the **Wow 7-Gradients** folder) that you can use in your own Styles, in Gradient Fill layers, or with the Gradient tool to make backgrounds or multicolor tints
- **More than 150 seamlessly tiling Pattern Presets** (in the **Wow 7-Patterns** folder) that can be used as fills and Fill layers or as Strokes, Overlays, or Textures in customizing or creating Layer Styles.

*Once installed, the **Wow 7-Patterns Presets** are available to any Photoshop dialog box or palette that uses Patterns.*

▶ *The "see also" eye 👁 points out related sections of the book, in case you need more information. For instance:* 👁 *See "Scaling a Style" on page 10–11 to learn about the important relationship between Layer Styles and the Resolution setting.*

▶ *You can use a Wow Style to "harmonize" a series of photos.*

*Here the **Wow-Tint FX 11** Style not only created a romantic mood, but also overcame differences in color and tone to instantly unify this wedding collage.*

▌n this *Adobe Photoshop 7 One-Click Wow!* book you'll find these sections that show you how to use the contents of the CD:

- Turn to "**One-Click Wow! Quick Start**" on pages 3–5 to learn how to install the **Wow 7-Styles** and other **Wow Presets**, and how to apply a Style.

- "**Layer Style 'Magic,'**" starting on page 9, begins by demonstrating how flexible and easy-to-use Styles are. Also included in "Layer Style 'Magic'" are tips for "**Scaling a Style**" once you've applied it (pages 10–11); "**Customizing Styles**" so you can modify them and then easily apply them again later (pages 12–13), "**Copying & Pasting Styles**" to apply the same Style to other photos, type, or graphics (page 14); "**Using Styles with Masks & Clipping Groups**" for styling images "framed" within a shape or type (pages 15–16), and "**Working with Styles in ImageReady**" (page 17).

*You can customize any **Wow Style** by applying it and then making changes in the Layer Styles dialog box. Here the Size setting for Bevel And Emboss was scaled up from its original 7 pixels (left) to 70 pixels, to change the "carving" without changing the wood grain, lighting, or Shadow.*

- "**Saving, Sizing & Output**" (pages 18–21) shows how to make a file the right size and format for printing, posting on the Web, or attaching to an email.

- "**A Layer Style Tutorial**" (pages 22–26) walks you step-by-step through working with Styles in Photoshop and ImageReady. The **Wow-Styles Tutorial** files needed for

working along with the steps are provided on the CD-ROM.

- Pages 27–77 include "**Gallery**" sections to inspire you, as well as printed samples of the Layer Styles provided on the CD. These examples are organized in two sections — "**Styles for Photos**" (pages 27–45) and "**Styles for Type & Graphics**" (pages 46–77), including "**Button Rollover Styles**" (on page 77).

- Page 78 introduces the four kinds of Wow Presets other than Styles, with tips for using the **Wow 7–Crop and Marquee Presets** and the **Wow 7-Pattern Presets**.

- "**How To Paint with the Wow! Paint & Clone Presets**" (on pages 79–81) tells how to work with the **Wow-Pattern Stamp, Art History**, and **Art Media Presets**, with suggestions for when to choose each of these three matched sets of artists' tools. The "**Painting Gallery**" and "**Pattern Stamp and Art History Presets**" (pages 82–85) show the results you can get by combining the cloning Presets with matching **Wow-Texture Styles** (shown on pages 44–45).

- "**Using the Wow! Image Fix Brushes**" (page 87) not only shows how to use these retouching brushes, but also suggests how to improve the overall tone, color, and condition of your photos before you begin the retouching process.

*Correcting "red-eye" is just one of the things you can do with the **Wow-Image Fix Brushes**.*

- "**Using the Wow! Actions**" (page 87) and the Actions samples that follow it (pages 88–89) provide instructions and examples for these "try 'em, you'll like 'em" routines.

- "**Gradients**" (page 90) is a one-page "catalog" of all the **Wow 7-Gradient Presets**.

ONE-CLICK WOW! QUICK START

Can't wait to get started? Here's how to get going right away.

▶ **One of the benefits of Layer Styles is that they are just as easy to "un-apply" — leaving your image untouched — as they are to apply in the first place. But if, in addition to applying Styles, you also plan to do some experimenting that could compromise your original image, it's a good idea to duplicate the image before you start your Photoshop work. After you open the file (File > Open), choose Image > Duplicate and click "OK" in the Duplicate Image dialog box. Then operate on the duplicate and keep the untouched original safe.**

To install and use the **One-Click Wow! Layer Styles** and other Presets, you'll need to **first install Adobe Photoshop.** Then follow the numbered steps below.

1 Installing the One-Click Wow! Styles and other Presets. Insert the One-Click Wow! CD-ROM into your computer's CD-ROM drive **and double-click its icon**, or use My Computer (Windows); locate and **copy the Wow 7-Styles folder into Photoshop 7's Styles folder** (inside the Presets folder).

Photoshop 7's Styles folder is inside the Presets folder.

Putting the One-Click Wow! Styles in this location will make them available to both Photoshop 7 and ImageReady 7.

While you're installing things, you can also copy the other Wow Presets into their corresponding Presets folders:

Finding the folders for the other Wow goodies

2 Starting up the Adobe Photoshop program. If Photoshop is already running, you'll need to quit the program and start it again so it can "find" the **One-Click Wow! Styles** and other Presets that you've added to the Styles folder and the various other Presets folders.

For convenience in working with Styles, be sure to have both the Layers palette and the Styles palette open. To open the Layers palette, **choose Window > Layers.** Open the Styles palette the same way (**choose Window > Styles**).

So that you can see the full names of the Styles, along with thumbnails large enough to see what the Styles look like, click the **little triangle in the upper right corner of the Styles palette and choose Large List from the pop-out menu.**

Photoshop 7's Styles palette — open in Large List mode

3 Preparing the file for working with One-Click Wow! Styles. Now open a file that you want to "style" (**choose File > Open**). You can duplicate the file for safekeeping if you like; see the tip at the left.

So that you'll get good results right away when you apply a **One-Click Wow! Style** to the file, change the Resolution setting for the file as follows: **Choose Image > Image Size;** in the Image Size dialog box, **make sure the "Resample Image" option is OFF** (no check mark in the box). **Then double-click to select the number in the Resolution setting box and type in 225; click "OK"** to close the Image Size box.

Changing the Resolution setting to 225 pixels/inch

4 Applying a Style. To target the layer where you want to apply a One-Click Wow! **Style, click the layer's name in the Layers palette.** (As the tip at the left explains, you can't apply a Style to the *Background*.)

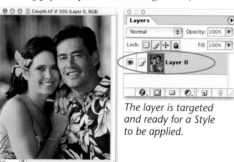

The layer is targeted and ready for a Style to be applied.

To apply one of the **One-Click Wow! Styles** to the targeted layer, first **click the triangle in the upper right corner of the Styles palette and choose the library of Styles you want from the list at the bottom of the pop-out menu.** (To get a good look at the contents of each library so you can decide which

▶ *If you try to apply a Style to a Background layer, nothing will happen. To convert a Background to a non-Background layer so that a Style can be applied, double-click the "Background" name in the Layers palette; then in the New Layer dialog box, click "OK."*

First double-click here.

Then click here.

one you want to choose, check the examples on pages 32–45 and 52–75 of this book.)

*Choosing the **Wow 7-01 Edge Styles** set*

In the "caution" box that appears, for now it's safest to click "Append," so that you don't accidentally delete any Styles that may currently be in the Styles palette but haven't yet been saved as part of a Styles library. ◉ *See the tip on page 23 for an explanation of when to append Styles to the palette and when to replace the current Styles.*

"Append" adds the Styles library you chose to the current list; "OK" replaces the current Styles.

With the **Wow 07-01 Edge Styles** loaded into the Styles palette, click the particular Style you want to apply.

*Choosing the **Wow-Edges 08** Style*

ONE-CLICK WOW! QUICK START *continued*

▶ *Although both Photoshop and ImageReady have Styles palettes, appending or replacing Styles in one program's palette doesn't affect the Styles palette in the other program. Each program's Styles palette has to be "stocked" with Styles separately.*

▶ *Photoshop and its Web-design companion Image-Ready are equipped with little context-sensitive labels called "Tool Tips." In either program if you pause the cursor over some part of the interface, a Tool Tip will pop up to identify the item under the cursor. You can turn the Tool Tips function on or off by choosing Edit > Preferences > General and clicking in the "Show Tool Tips" box.*

👁 *See "Working with Styles in ImageReady" on page 17 and step 10 of "A Layer Style Tutorial" on page 26 for pointers on using Styles in ImageReady.*

The Style will be applied to your file instantly! You'll see the result in the working window, and in the Layers palette an 𝒇 icon appears next to the layer name.

*The **Wow-Edges 08** Style applied*

👁 *See pages 10–21 for pointers on working with Styles in Photoshop, and pages 22–26 for a step-by-step tutorial.*

Getting started with Styles in Image-Ready. To work with Styles in ImageReady (Photoshop's companion Web-design program), start up the program from the desktop or by clicking the "Jump to ImageReady" button at the very bottom of Photoshop's Tools palette. Once ImageReady is open, any Styles libraries that you've loaded into Photoshop's Styles folder as described in step 1 on page 3 will also be available to ImageReady's Styles palette.

To get started working with Styles, make sure the Layers palette and Styles palette are open (**Window > Layers** and **Window > Styles**). To see the name and thumbnail for each Style in the palette, **click the little triangle** near the top right corner of the palette and **choose Small List**.

The **Wow 7-20 Button Styles** library was designed especially for use with ImageReady. To load this library, choose it from the Styles palette's pop-out menu. To apply a particular **Wow-Button Style, click the target layer's name** in the Layers palette, then **click on a Wow Style** in the Styles palette.

In ImageReady's Styles palette, even in the tiny thumbnails of Small List mode, you can see a black triangle in the upper left corner of each Rollover Style. A Rollover Style makes on-screen buttons change in response to what the user does.

As in Photoshop, the Style will be applied to your file instantly, and the 𝒇 icon will appear next to the layer's name in the Layers palette. If the Style you've applied is a Rollover, the slice icon 🖈 will also appear, between the layer's name and the 𝒇, to show that the Rollover Style has automatically created a rectangular area that will respond when the cursor enters or leaves it.

Four "Rollover-styled" buttons in ImageReady. Each button is on its own layer and has a different Rollover Style applied to it. The boundaries of the slices show in the working window.

To see a "Rollover-styled" button in action after you've applied the Style, click the Preview Document tool near the bottom of the Tools palette to put the file into Preview mode. Then move the cursor into the slice to see the Over state and click to see the Down state.

Click on the Preview Document tool to test the Rollover Style you've applied.

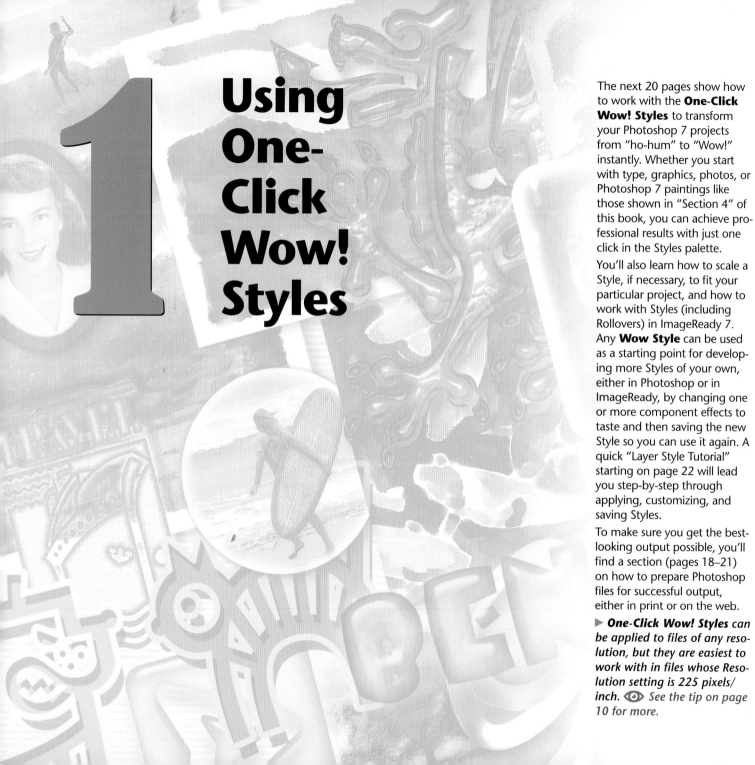

Using One-Click Wow! Styles

1

The next 20 pages show how to work with the **One-Click Wow! Styles** to transform your Photoshop 7 projects from "ho-hum" to "Wow!" instantly. Whether you start with type, graphics, photos, or Photoshop 7 paintings like those shown in "Section 4" of this book, you can achieve professional results with just one click in the Styles palette.

You'll also learn how to scale a Style, if necessary, to fit your particular project, and how to work with Styles (including Rollovers) in ImageReady 7. Any **Wow Style** can be used as a starting point for developing more Styles of your own, either in Photoshop or in ImageReady, by changing one or more component effects to taste and then saving the new Style so you can use it again. A quick "Layer Style Tutorial" starting on page 22 will lead you step-by-step through applying, customizing, and saving Styles.

To make sure you get the best-looking output possible, you'll find a section (pages 18–21) on how to prepare Photoshop files for successful output, either in print or on the web.

▶ *One-Click Wow! Styles can be applied to files of any resolution, but they are easiest to work with in files whose Resolution setting is 225 pixels/ inch.* ◉ *See the tip on page 10 for more.*

WHAT IS A LAYER STYLE?

A Style is a way to improve photos, type, or graphics — instantly! — by "overlaying" color, texture, dimension, framing or any of a dozen other effects.

▶ *The Layer Styles and other Presets on the **Adobe Photoshop 7 One-Click Wow! CD-ROM** were designed as indispensable tools for Photoshop 7 and ImageReady 7. The Layer Styles, Patterns, and Gradients work beautifully in Photoshop 6 and ImageReady 3. However, the Tool Presets (new with Photoshop 7) and Actions (because of Photoshop 7 interface changes) are not compatible with Photoshop 6.*

*A separate book-and-CD-ROM package — **Adobe Photoshop Elements One-Click Wow!** (Davis and Dayton, Peachpit Press) — has Styles and instructions specifically adapted for Adobe Photoshop Elements.*

Simply stated, a Layer Style is a "look" that you can add to photos, type, or graphics *instantly* — simply by clicking in the Styles palette. Below are a few of the highly sophisticated kinds of effects you can apply with the Styles from the **One-Click Wow! CD-ROM.** To create such a treatment *without* using Layer Styles could take a lot of time, work, and skill, as shown at the right.

*A Style can be a color treatment such as a "partial sepiatone" (**Wow-Tint FX 01**) or an exaggeration of color and contrast (**Wow-Darkroom 04**).*

*A Style can provide edge effects for photos, such as a modern border treatment (**Wow-Edges 05**) or an antique wooden frame (**Wow-Frame 05**).*

*A Style can turn plain type or graphics into convincing material objects, such as chiseled steel (**Wow-Metals 17**) or transparent blue plastic (**Wow-Plastic 08**).*

At the Wow! intergalactic headquarters, we've used the following "ingredients" to cook up the **One-Click Wow! Layer Styles:**

- A **drop shadow,** sharp or soft
- An **inner shadow** that extends inward from the edge of the artwork, which can produce a "carved" effect
- Light or dark **glows** that extend inward or outward from the edges of the art
- A **beveled edge,** wide or narrow, sharp or rounded
- An **overlay** of a single color, a gradient, or a pattern that changes or even replaces the original color of a photo, type, or graphic
- An **opacity** control that can make the "styled" artwork partly or fully transparent
- A **texture** that creates bumps and pits on the surface of the artwork
- A **stroke** — even a multicolor stroke — that outlines the edges of the art
- A "satin" treatment that can add sophisticated reflection and refraction effects

*With a Layer Style (**Wow-Gems 02**), you can turn a solid gray circle into the gemstone lozenge above. Or you can achieve the same result without a Style, by building the 11-layer file at the right, with the original circle serving as the base of a clipping group. The choice is a "no-brainer"!*

Bevel shadow

Bevel highlight

Inner shadow

Inner glow

"Satin" effect

Color overlay

Pattern overlay

Original gray circle

Outer glow

Drop shadow

Background

*When the visitor clicks the button, the **Down** state appears, signaling that the click has been noted and something will now happen.*

In ImageReady 7, Styles can be used in all the same ways they can be used in Photoshop 7. But in addition, ImageReady can use *Rollover Styles,* which provide the "on-screen activity" for buttons on Web pages and other interactive interfaces. These Rollovers provide the color, dimension, and JavaScript programming that make on-screen buttons change, depending on what the user is doing. The **Wow Button** Styles that have the words "All Three" in their names are Rollover Styles. Found in the **Wow 7-20 Button Styles** library, they have three states:

*The **Normal** state is the way the button looks as it sits and waits for a Web site visitor to interact with it.*

*When the site visitor moves the cursor over the button, the **Over** state brings the button to life. The change from Normal to Over is designed to catch the eye, signaling that clicking the button will make something happen.*

The **Wow Button-All Three** Styles provide a wide range of options for the Normal state, as shown in the examples below on the left. The Over state often lights up the button or changes its color. And the Down state typically makes the button look "pushed," closer to the surface it sits on, or even depressed slightly below the surface.

Normal   Over   Down

▶ *Each of the One-Click Wow! Rollover Styles has built-in JavaScript code that changes the look of the buttons in response to the cursor. If you're curious about the code, you can click the "Preview in Default Browser" button at the bottom of ImageReady's Tools palette and read it.*

LAYER STYLE "MAGIC"

After you apply a Style, it's easy to make changes to the layer content or to the Style itself.

▶ *To remove a Layer Style from a layer, you can right-click (Windows) or Ctrl-click (Mac) the* ⓕ *icon next to the layer's name in the Layers palette to open a context-sensitive menu, where you can* **choose Clear Layer Style***. Or click the "Clear Style" button at the bottom of the Styles palette:*

Layer Styles are extremely flexible! Once you've applied a Style, **you can change the content of the layer and the Layer Style will conform to the changes.**

If you apply a Style (here **Wow-Metals 06***) to a type layer and then change the font, the Style is retained.*

You can even edit the text, and the Style will conform to the new wording.

If you reshape your graphics, the Style (here **Wow-Metals 19** *with its beveled edge and highlighting) conforms to the new shape.*

If you paint or draw on a layer that already has a Style applied to it, the Style (here **Wow-Plastic 07***) will automatically be added to each new stroke as you create it.*

Not only can you change the content of a "styled" layer (as shown in the examples at the left), but **you can also completely replace the Style or change its individual attributes.**

Here the **Wow-Chrome 10** *Style was applied (bottom) completely replacing* **Wow-Metals 06***.*

In ImageReady, Rollover Styles and the layer-based slices associated with them also conform to the shape of the layer content, so **you can transform a button's shape and still retain the Style,** including the rollover interactivity.

The **Wow Button 03-All Three** *Rollover Style was applied to four identical buttons on four different layers. Shown here is the Normal state, with the bounding boxes for the interactive slices.*

When the button graphics were stretched, the Style conformed to the new shape, and the slices were automatically redrawn to fit.

Scaling a Style

To "custom-fit" a Layer Style to a particular file, try scaling the Style.

▶ *Each Layer Style "remembers" the Resolution setting of the Photoshop file in which it was created. The **One-Click Wow! Styles** were created in files with a Resolution setting of 225 pixels/inch. Although these Styles can be applied to files of any resolution, they are easiest to work with if you first make sure the Resolution setting for your file is 225 pixels/inch. You can do this — without altering your image at all — by choosing **Image** > **Image Size**, then making sure* "Resample Image" is turned OFF, *and typing in "225" for the Resolution setting, as explained in step 3 of "One-Click Wow! Quick Start" on pages 3–4.*

After you apply a Layer Style, there's a good chance you'll want to scale it. That's because a Style can look different depending on whether you apply it to a thick or thin graphic, a bold or light-weight typeface, or a large or small photo.

1 Applying the Style. The first step is to **apply a Layer Style** as described in "One-Click Wow! Quick Start" on pages 3–5 or in "Copying & Pasting Styles" on page 14.

Great Grandma's portrait needs a frame.

*But the frame and mat applied by the **Wow-Frame 03** Style (page 34) seem to cover up too much of the photo. The Style needs to be scaled.*

2 Scaling. **Right-click (Windows) or Ctrl-click (Mac) on the** ⓕ **icon** to the right of the styled layer's name in the Layers palette, and **choose Scale Effects from the context-sensitive menu that pops out.** In the Scale Layer Effects dialog box, to pop out the Scale slider, **click the little triangle** to the left of the "%" sign. **Move the slider** until the Layer Style looks right. Or type in a specific percentage, according to the suggestions in the **Note** below.

Using the context-sensitive menu to open the Scale Layer Effects dialog box (above left) and scaling the Style to 50% (above) improves the framing.

Note: There are some important options to consider when you apply a Layer Style that includes a pattern or texture effect:

- First, certain Scale percentages work best for keeping the surface markings or texture of a Layer Style sharp and clear. (Each **One-Click Wow! Style** that includes a pattern or texture has an **asterisk [*]** after its name in the examples shown on pages 32–45 and 52–75 of this book.) If you've made sure that the Resolution setting of your file is 225 pixels/inch (as described in the tip on page 10), these optimal percentages are 25%, 50%, 100% (no scaling), and 200%. If none of these percentages is ideal for your project, you may need to accept a somewhat soft-looking pattern in order to get the ideal width of the frame, for instance. (Styles that *don't* include a surface pattern or texture don't have an asterisk in their names, and you don't have to worry about restricting the Scale setting to one of these values.)

*Scaling the **Wow-Frame 03** Style to 48% blurs the pattern (top), but using a Scale factor of exactly 50% keeps the pattern sharp.*

- Second, when you reduce the Scale of a patterned or textured Style, **the repeat in the pattern may become more apparent.** For instance, if you look carefully at the frame around Great Grandma's portrait in step 2 on page 10, you can see that the repeating pattern that's used to create the texture is more obvious than it was in step 1, when the Style was first applied at the default 100% Scale setting. In this case we chose to allow the repeat to show in order to get the right width for the frame, since the repeat wasn't distracting.

If you apply a **One-Click Wow! Style** to **a file whose Resolution is** *not* **set to 225 pixels/ inch,** you may get a result that looks different from the corresponding sample shown in this

▶ *It's possible to scale a Layer Style so small that some of its features go away — for instance, the bevel or drop shadow could disappear if you were to set a very low Scale value in the Scale Effects dialog box and then click OK to close the box. Once you've scaled a file too small, you may not be able to successfully scale it up again. If that happens, you can simply apply the Style again and scale again, this time not as small.*

book. Here are some examples of **Wow-Frame 03** applied to exactly the same file but with four different, commonly used Resolution settings:

72 pixels/inch

150 pixels/inch

225 pixels/inch

300 pixels/inch

Note that changing a file's Resolution in order to scale a Style isn't an efficient approach. Instead, it's much more effective to use the scaling method described in step 2 starting on page 10. But if you apply a **One-Click Wow! Style** to a file whose Resolution is *not* set at 225 pixels/inch, here are some settings you can use in the Scale Layer Effects dialog box in order to help keep it sharp if it has a pattern. The percentages in bold type will produce the same results as the default 100% Scale in a 225 pixels/inch file. (Again, for Styles without a surface pattern or texture, you don't have to worry about using these special Scale settings.)

72 pixels/inch: 78%, 156%, **312%**, 624%
150 pixels/inch: 75%, **150%**, 300%
300 pixels/inch: 75%, 150%, 300%

Customizing Styles

Photoshop lets you change the component effects of a Style you've applied, or even add more effects. Then you can save your customized Style for future use.

▶ *The aim of this book is to show what can be done with the Presets on the One-Click Wow! CD-ROM, and to explain how to use them. For complete coverage of Layer Styles, including how to create them from scratch and how to work with the Blending Options, we recommend the most recent edition of The Photoshop Wow! Book, especially the chapter on "Special Effects for Type & Graphics."*

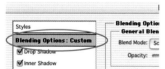

In addition to the effects, a Layer Style includes Blending Options that control how the Style and the layer interact with other layers and with masks.

If you don't find *exactly* the Layer Style you want among the **One-Click Wow! Styles**, you can apply one that's close to what you want and then modify it. The Layer Style dialog box is where you make changes to a Style after you've applied it to a layer.

You can open the Layer Style dialog box (below) by double-clicking the ● to the right of the "styled" layer's name in the Layers palette or by double-clicking any of the effects in the expanded list underneath.

On the left side of the Layer Style dialog box are listed all the effects that can be included in a Style. Those that are actually included in the current Style have check marks in the boxes next to their names. You can add or delete an effect by clicking its check box. Clicking the name of the effect turns on the effect and opens the appropriate section of the Layer Style box so you can customize it.

To customize an effect, it helps to know what that effect does. Here's a brief intro:

• The **Shadows** and **Glows** add soft darkening or lightening effects around the edges of whatever the layer contains. You can change whether they are dark or light by changing their color and Blend Mode. You can also adjust their softness or density. Two characteristics can't be changed:

(1) The **Drop Shadow** and **Outer Glow** extend **outward** from the edge, but the **Inner Shadow** and **Inner Glow** extend **inward**; and (2) the Glows always **extend evenly** in all directions, whereas the **Shadows can be offset.**

The Wow-Frame 07 Style includes a typical dark Drop Shadow.   *In Wow-Glow 02 a bright purple Drop Shadow in Screen mode adds to the neon glow.*

• The settings in the **Bevel And Emboss** section of the Layer Style box interact to create beveled edges, and the settings in the **Contour** and **Texture** "subeffects" can also contribute. The **Contour** is important in shaping the "shoulder" of the bevel, and the **Texture** can add surface "bump."

 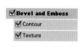

In Wow-Metal 15 the Contour helps shape the edge, and the Texture makes the surface bumpy.

• The **Satin** effect can add complex "interior" lighting in a translucent Style or reflections in an opaque Style.

Wow-Plastic 09 with its built-in Satin effect turned on (left) to create refracted light and turned off (right)   *In Wow-Chrome 20 the built-in Satin effect simulates reflections (left); turning Satin off dulls the chrome.*

• **Overlay** effects apply **Color**, **Gradient**, and **Pattern**, which are "stacked" in that top-to-bottom order if more than one is applied.

▶ *With the Layer Style dialog box open to a particular effect's section, there are some things you can change without using the sliders or typing numbers — just by dragging the cursor in your image. For instance, you can drag to change the Angle and offset Distance of a Drop Shadow or an Inner Shadow, or to reposition the Texture subeffect, the Satin effect, the Gradient Overlay or Pattern Overlay, or the coloring for most kinds of Gradient- or Pattern-based Strokes.*

▶ *Besides changing the individual component effects in a Style, you can also scale all the effects in the Style together, or resize an entire "styled" file, keeping all the Styles in proportion, as described in "**Scaling a Style**" on pages 10–11.*

▶ *Clicking the "Styles" button at the top of the list in the Layer Style dialog box opens the current Styles palette — right inside the box!*

*In **Wow-Woods 15** the Pattern Overlay creates the wood-grain (left), the Gradient Overlay in Color Dodge mode adds lighting (center), and a dark yellow Color Overlay in Overlay mode subtly enhances color and contrast.*

- The **Stroke** effect outlines the edges with Color, a Gradient, or even a Pattern. The stroke can be inside, outside, or straddling the edge.

*The neon tubing of **Wow-Glow 01** is created with a Shape Burst gradient Stroke.*

O nce you've applied a Style, you can make changes in the Layer Style box to modify it. Here are just a few examples:

- You can make an element look farther "above" the surface simply by increasing the Distance of the Drop Shadow.

*In the **Wow-Fabric 16** Style, increasing the Drop Shadow effect's Distance setting from the built-in 9 px (pixels) (left) to 36 px makes the type seem to float higher above the page.*

- You can change the lighting direction by changing the Angle setting for the Drop Shadow, Inner Shadow, and Bevel And Emboss. (If you change one of these, you'll need to change all of them in order to keep the Style's lighting consistent.)

*Changing the Angle for the Drop Shadow effect in **Wow-Chrome 13** from the built-in 120 degrees (left) to –60 degrees (right) changes the light source from upper left to lower right.*

- You can change the molding of a picture frame Style by choosing a different Contour in the Contour subeffect's section.

*Changing from the relatively simple built-in Contour used for the Contour subeffect of Bevel And Emboss (left) to a more complex Contour (right) changes the molding of the frame created by **Wow-Frame 04**.*

- In a Style that uses the same Pattern choice for the Pattern Overlay and the Texture subeffect, you can smooth the surface by turning off the Texture.

*The **Wow-Plastic 03** Style with its built-in Texture subeffect (left) and without it (right)*

A fter you've made changes to a Style, you can save it for future use. First add it to the current Styles palette. Then use the Preset Manager to save it as part of a Styles library.
👁 *See step 8 of "A Layer Style Tutorial" on page 25 for directions for naming and saving Styles.*

Copying & Pasting Styles

Styles can be copied from layer to layer or even file to file.

▶ *When you copy a Style from one file and paste it to another, you're much more likely to get the same "look" if the two files have the same Resolution setting. (Remember, all the **One-Click Wow! Styles** except the **Wow-Button Styles** were created at a standard 225 pixels/inch.) A quick way to find a file's Resolution is to Alt/Option-click the description entry in the lower left corner of the working window.*

If the Resolution settings of your files are different and you need to temporarily change the Resolution setting of the "recipient" file to match that of the "donor," choose Image > Image Size, make sure "Resample Image" is turned OFF, and type in the Resolution setting from the donor file. (You can follow the same procedure to reset the Resolution back to its original value after you paste the Style.)

It's easy to copy a Style from one layer and apply it to other layers, in the same file or a different one. This makes it possible to reproduce a Style that you create "from scratch" or one that you find already applied in a file. Here's how you can go about copying and pasting a Style:

1 To copy a Style, right-click (Windows) or Ctrl-click (Mac) on the 𝑓 icon to the right of the layer's name to open a context-sensitive menu where you can choose Copy Layer Style. (Another option is to **choose Layer > Layer Style > Copy Layer Style**.)

We liked the Style that we found on the "Dinner" layer of this photo collage (it's a scaled version of Wow-Edges 05), and we wanted to apply it to other layers.

We used the context-sensitive menu to copy the Style.

2 To paste the copied Style, right-click (Windows) or Ctrl-click (Mac) to the right of the name of a layer where you want to apply the Style. The context-sensitive menu will open again, and you can **choose Paste Layer Style**.

We pasted the copied Style to another layer, again using the context-sensitive menu.

3 Continue pasting to any other layers where you want to apply the Style. If you want to copy and paste a Style to more than two layers, you can save time by "linking" these target layers together and then pasting the copied Style to all of them at once:

To link layers together, in the Layers palette click on the thumbnail of one of them. Then click in the column just to the left of the thumbnail for each of the other layers you want to link to it. For each layer you link, a link icon will appear in the column.

Once the layers are linked, use the context-sensitive menu again, but this time choose **Paste Layer Style To Linked**.

Several layers were linked, and the copied Style was pasted to all of them at once. The shared Style helps unify the six assembled images.

Using Styles with Masks & Clipping Groups

Layer masks, vector masks, and clipping groups provide a way to mask an image inside any shape or type.

▶ **In Photoshop 7 there are some new ways to add a vector mask to a layer. First target the layer in the Layers palette.**

• **Then you can use the main menu — choose Layer > Add Vector Mask.**

• **Or you can Ctrl/⌘-click the "Add a mask" button at the bottom of the palette.**

• **If you've already added a layer mask to the layer, Photoshop is smart enough to know that a vector mask is the only masking option that's left. So you can leave out the Ctrl/⌘ and simply click the "Add a mask" button.**

In Photoshop, each layer (except *Background*) can have two masks — a pixel-based *layer mask* and an outline-based *vector mask*. These masks determine which parts of the layer will show and which will be hidden.

You can add a vector mask to a layer by Ctrl/⌘-clicking the "Add a mask" button at the bottom of the Layers palette. Then choose a Shape tool (such as the Ellipse) from the Tools palette, click the "Add to path area (+)" button in the Options bar, and drag to draw the mask.

By default, a layer mask or vector mask is linked to the layer content. So, for example, if you drag the image with the Move tool, its mask will move also, and the same area of the image will remain showing. But if you break the link by clicking the link icon between the image thumbnail and mask thumbnail, then when you move the image, the mask will stay stationary, and a different part of the image will be revealed.

When the link is broken between an image and its mask as shown here, you can reposition the image inside the mask by dragging with the Move tool in the working window.

When a "styled" layer has either kind of mask, by default any edge effects in the Style will follow the edges of the mask.

*The **Wow-Tint FX 03** Style creates a partial sepiatone and also adds an interior glow and a drop shadow around the edges. Our vector mask serves as the edge to which the glow is applied.*

If you modify the mask, as shown below, the Style conforms to the new shape.

The ellipse was reshaped to hold both people by choosing the Path Selection tool (the solid arrow just above the Pen in the Tools palette), pressing Ctrl/⌘-T, and dragging a corner of the box.

You can turn *off* a mask's influence on *edge effects* by turning *on* "Layer Mask Hides Effects" or "Vector Mask Hides Effects" in the Blending Options section of the Layer Styles dialog box.

Turning on "Vector Mask Hides Effects" in the Blending Options section of the Layer Style dialog box hides the glow and shadow.

continued on page 16

Using Styles with Masks & Clipping Groups

continued

▶ **When you want to make a clipping group from layers that are stacked up in your Photoshop file, there are several ways to go about it:**

- **In the Layers palette you can target the layer above your soon-to-be "clipping" layer and then from Photoshop's main menu choose Layer > Group With Previous.**

- **Or target the layer and use the keyboard shortcut for Group With Previous, which is Ctrl/⌘-G.**

- **You can hold down the Alt/Option key and move the cursor into the Layers palette, positioning it over the border between the "clipping" layer and the layer above it. When the cursor changes to the double-circle clipping icon, click to form the clipping group.**

You can add more layers to a clipping group simply by working sequentially up the stack of layers in the Layers palette, using any of the methods above.

A *clipping group* allows you to use the content of one layer as a mask for a different layer (or layers) above it. 👁 *See the tip at the left for three methods for forming a clipping group.* When you create a clipping group, in the Layers palette the name of the "cookie cutter" (clipping) layer is underlined, and the name of the clipped layer is indented.

Using a clipping group can have certain advantages over using a layer mask or vector mask. One advantage is that with a clipping group you can mask an image inside type and still keep the type "live" and editable.

*You can make a clipping group by Alt/Option-clicking between layers as shown here. Any Style applied to the "clipping" layer will also apply to the "clipped" layer above it. In this case the **Wow-Glass 12** Style was applied to the "Seaside" type layer.*

By default, in a clipping group if you move (or scale or rotate) the "clipped" layer, the "clipping" layer below doesn't move with it. This makes it easy to reposition the clipped image inside the clipping type or shape.

The image was rotated inside the type by clicking on the photo layer in the Layers palette, then pressing Ctrl/⌘-T (for Edit > Free Transform) and dragging clockwise on a corner handle of the Transform box.

However, if you want to move (or scale or rotate) the whole clipping group, you can do so by first linking its layers: In the Layers palette, target any layer in the group; then, for any other layer you want to link to the targeted layer, click in the column to the right of the "eye"; you'll see a link icon appear in this column. Once the layers are linked, moving, rotating, or scaling any one of them will affect them all together.

The photo layer was targeted and the "Seaside" type layer was linked to it. Then the Free Transform command was used to rotate both layers together.

Another advantage of making a clipping group is that you can use it to mask (and "style") more than one layer.

*Each of the six photos in this collage (above left) is on a separate layer. All of the layers were added to a clipping group with an Ellipse Shape layer as its base (clipping) layer, and the **Wow-Tint FX 08** Style was applied to this layer. The Style affects all of the "clipped" photos, adding a slight tint and a "pebbled" surface texture and darkening their clipped edges.*

Working with Styles in Image-Ready

Use Styles in ImageReady to add dimension and interactivity to button graphics.

▶ **In ImageReady, by default the list of individual effects in a Style is not displayed in the Layers palette. Click the little triangle to the left of the *f* icon to show the list.**

▶ **Rollover Styles are designed to be used in ImageReady. If you apply a Rollover Style in Photoshop, only the Normal state will be applied and it will not be interactive.**

▶ **It's a good idea to keep button labels on a separate layer from the button graphics. That way you can keep the type "live" and even give the type layer a separate "single" Style of its own.**

In ImageReady 7 you load and apply Styles just as you do in Photoshop 7. But in addition to the "single" Styles you can apply in Photoshop, in ImageReady you can also apply and customize *Rollover Styles.*

In the **Wow 7-20 Button Styles** library (designed especially for use in ImageReady), the Styles whose names include the words "**All Three**" are Rollover Styles.

To apply a Style in ImageReady, choose a Styles library from the Styles palette's pop-out menu, target a layer in the Layers palette, and then click the Style you want in the Styles palette. (Rollover Styles have a small black mark in the upper left corner of the thumbnail.)

When you apply one of the **Wow Button-All Three** Styles to a layer, an interactive rectangular *slice* is created, big enough to include everything in the styled layer that isn't transparent. The slice automatically responds to what the user does with the cursor. Each **Wow Button-All Three** Style has **Normal, Over,** and **Down** states. *See "What Is a Layer Style?" on page 8 for definitions of these three states.*

*Applying **Wow Button-All Three** Styles to three buttons, each in its own layer, created a layer-based slice for each graphic.*

ImageReady 7's Rollovers palette makes it easy to target a particular state in a Rollover Style you've applied, so you can examine it or make changes. For instance:

- To view (and target) a particular state, click on its name in the Rollovers palette.

In the Rollovers palette, click the little triangle to the left of the Normal State's entry to show the other states in the Rollover. Click on a particular state's thumbnail to target that state.

- To replace the Style used for the targeted state, you can click a single (non-Rollover) Style in the Styles palette.

- To edit one or more effects of the targeted state's Style, target the appropriate layer in the Layers palette, then double-click the name of the effect in the Layers palette to open that effect's palette. (Single-state Styles can also be customized this way.)

There's more to an Image Ready effects palette than meets the eye. Clicking on the ◆ toggle on a palette's title tab expands the palette (right) to make all of its controls available.

- To keep the Style but change the state it represents, double-click the name of the state and choose from the Rollover State Options dialog box.

Choosing a different state

SAVING, SIZING & OUTPUT

For maximum flexibility, save your layered and "styled" file in Photoshop format. Then choose the right size and file format for output for:

- *printing directly from Photoshop,*
- *placing your image in another program for printing,*
- *doing further work to the file in ImageReady, or*
- *displaying the image on-screen.*

As you work on "styling" a file in Photoshop, it's a good idea to save the file periodically in the native Photoshop (.psd) format. This will keep "alive" and "editable" all the information that you build into the file — including type, layers and Layer Styles — so you can go back and make changes to them later if you like.

Saving your layered file. The first time you save your file, **choose File > Save As.** In the Save As dialog box, **choose Photoshop** for the Format; make sure the **"As a Copy" box is NOT checked** and the **"Layers" box IS checked,** so the layers and Layer Styles will be preserved. Name the file, choose where you want to store it, and then click the **"Save"** button.

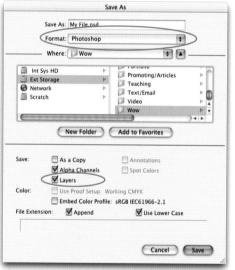

Photoshop 7's Save As dialog box (Mac OS X), set up for saving a layered file in the flexible Photoshop format

For subsequent saves as you work on the file, simply **choose File > Save** or **press Ctrl/⌘-S.** The file will be resaved in Photoshop format.

When you've finished applying and customizing Layer Styles and you've saved your finished file in Photoshop format, it's easy to get it sized for printing, as described next, and ready to print directly from Photoshop, or ready to place in a page layout or word-processing program. (If you want to do more work on your file in ImageReady, go to "Reducing a copy of the layered file for further work in ImageReady" on page 20. Or if you simply want to send your file as an email attachment or post it on a Web page, go to "Resizing for email or for the Web" on page 21.)

Whether you'll be printing directly from Photoshop or placing a file in another program and printing from there, you can use the Image Size dialog box to figure out whether you can get good results by printing the image "as is" or whether you'll need to change its dimensions before you print.

Checking the size of your file for printing. To open the Image Size dialog box, choose **Image > Image Size.** Make sure the "Resample Image" box is NOT checked. ◉ *The tip on page 19 tells why turning off "Resample Image" is important.*

If the size you want is different from the current Width and Height settings shown in the Document Size section of the box, **type in the Width or Height** value you want. The other dimension will change automatically to keep the image in proportion, and the **Resolution** setting will change also.

If the new Resolution setting is *at least* as high as one of the following, your file has plenty of information for printing at the size you've entered. As a rule of thumb:

- A safe Resolution setting for inkjet printing is **150 pixels/inch** or higher.
- A safe Resolution setting for commercial **printing on a press** is **225 pixels/inch** or higher.

▶ *With "Resample Image" turned OFF in the Image Size dialog box, **none of the changes you make in the dialog box will change the color of any of the pixels** (the square dots that make up the image file). For example, if you **reduce the Width and Height dimensions,** the Resolution setting will increase. Basically, you are telling Photoshop to keep each of the pixels exactly the same color it is, but print all the pixels smaller. That way each one will take up less space and they can be packed more tightly to make a smaller, sharper printed image.*

*On the other hand, if you **increase the dimensions,** again the pixels aren't changed, but they will be printed larger. You just need to be careful that pixel size doesn't get so large — in other words Resolution (pixels/inch) doesn't get so low — that the pixels themselves can be seen, usually as jagged edges in areas of contrast.*

A file that doesn't have enough pixels/inch is likely to show pixel artifacts. This is especially likely when the image is printed on a press.

If your file's Resolution setting falls in one of these "safe" zones, you can proceed to "Printing directly from Photoshop" or " Preparing a duplicate file to place in another program" (both at the right).

Resizing the file for printing if you need to. If your file's Resolution setting is less than the appropriate "safe" value on page 18, it may not make a crisp and clean print.

The low Resolution value in the Image Size dialog box means that if this file were to be printed at 8 x 10 inches, the print might look "pixelated" (with visibly jagged edges).

An easy option for improving print quality is to raise the Resolution setting into the safe range by setting up the file to print smaller: Reduce the Width/Height dimensions until the Resolution rises to a safe number.

Reducing the Width and Height to 5 x 4 inches raised the Resolution setting high enough so this file could be printed on an inkjet printer.

By reducing the dimensions with "Resample Image" turned OFF, you are telling Photoshop to keep each pixel (tiny square dot) in the image exactly the same color but make all the pixels

print smaller so they can be packed tighter (more pixels/inch) on the printed page and the viewer's eye won't be able to detect the individual square dots in the printed image.

Printing directly from Photoshop.
Once your dimensions are set and your Resolution setting is safe, if you're printing directly from Photoshop, you're all set. All you have to do is **choose File > Print With Preview**, check the position of the image on the page, and **click Print** (or click Page Setup if you need to rotate the page orientation). Then make sure that your printer's options are set up to best match the paper you're using. Some printers also have advanced options for improving the print quality of photos or artwork.

The Epson C80's driver software can tell whether your image is color or black-and-white, but you have to tell it what kind of paper you're using (here photo-quality inkjet paper). This printer's PhotoEnhance mode works well for photos and many other images.

Preparing a duplicate file to place in another program. If your image will be placed in a page layout program and printed from there, you'll need to do just a little more work. One good way to prepare a file for printing from another program is to save a flattened copy (a *flattened* file is one that consists only of a single *Background* layer).

First, to make a duplicate copy to flatten, **choose Image > Duplicate.**

Duplicating the file

SAVING, SIZING & OUTPUT

continued

▶ *As a rule of thumb, here are some of the most useful file formats for saving projects in Photoshop:*

- *To keep all layers and Styles "alive" or to print an image from within Photoshop, save in **Photoshop** (or .psd) format.*

- *If your goal is to place the image on a page in a page layout program, **TIFF** (.tif) works well in most cases.*

- *Because it can reduce file size so effectively, **JPEG** (.jpg) is a good format for posting on the Web or for attaching to an email. Note that JPEG compression can cause a noticeable reduction in image quality.*

- *If you want your file to be readable with Adobe Acrobat Reader (a widely used free application that works on both Windows and Mac), save in **Photoshop PDF** (.pdf) format.*

*To read more about formats for saving files, in Photoshop 7 **choose Help > Photoshop Help** and **choose the "Saving and Exporting"** topic from the Contents; then **click on "About file formats."***

Then, to flatten this copy, **choose Layer > Flatten Image**. This will make a single-*Background*-layer version of your file. The image will look the same as the layered file, but the separate layers and Styles will no longer be available for changing. Transparency will be replaced with white, and type will no longer be "live." (That's why it was important to flatten a *copy* but also to save the original "live" file in Photoshop format as described in "Saving your layered file" on page 18.)

To save this duplicate file, **choose File > Save As** and select an appropriate format, such as **TIFF**, from the Format list in the Save As dialog box ◉ *See the tip at the left for help on choosing a file format.* Name the file, choose where you want to save it, and **click "Save."**

If, instead of being printed, your duplicate file will ultimately be displayed on the screen — for instance, as part of an animation or an interactive interface or as an attachment to email or an image for a Web page — you may want to reduce its pixel dimensions so the entire image will fit, even on a small screen.

Reducing a copy of the layered file for further work in ImageReady. You may want to bring a fully layered and "styled" version of your file into ImageReady so you can make buttons, or so you can turn various layers on and off in building an animation. If so, you'll want to preserve the Layer Styles by reducing the size of the file in Photoshop first: Make a duplicate of the layered file in Photoshop by choosing Image > Duplicate and clicking "OK."

Duplicating the file

What you must do next will seem a bit convoluted, but it's important to do it as described because of the strange and wonderful relationship between Photoshop's Layer Styles and the Resolution setting. The secret is to change the Resolution (pixels/inch setting), *not* the pixel dimensions:

1. Figure out a target pixel dimension for either Width or Height. For instance, you may need to make the file exactly 464 pixels high for a particular project.

2. **Working in the duplicate file,** open the Image Size dialog box (**Image > Image Size**). Turn "Resample Image" ON **and also** turn "Constrain Proportions" ON.

3. In the image Size dialog box change the Resolution setting — not the Height or Width setting — until the critical number (Height or Width) at the top of the box matches the target you figured out in step 1. You can use decimal fractions for the Resolution to arrive at exactly the right number of pixels for Height or Width.

Watch the "pixels" settings at the top of the dialog box as you use a trial-and-error method to arrive at a Resolution setting that will produce your target number of pixels for Width or Height (here 464 pixels).

4. Click "OK" to complete the resizing and close the dialog box. The image will have been resized, and any Styles in the file will have been scaled along with it.

To move the resized file to ImageReady 7, **click the "Jump to ImageReady" button** at the very bottom of Photoshop's Tools palette.

Resizing for email or for the Web. The difference between preparing a layered file for further work in ImageReady and preparing a file to be attached to email or posted on the Web is that you start by making a flattened, rather than layered, duplicate of your "styled" Photoshop file: **Choose Image > Duplicate,** click "OK," and then **choose Layer > Flatten Image.** ◉ See *"Preparing a duplicate file to place in another program" on page 19–20 for more about flattening a file.*

Working in the new flattened copy of the file, Open the Image Size dialog box (**choose Image > Image Size**). **Turn** "Resample Image" ON and also **turn** "Constrain Proportions" ON. In the **Pixel Dimensions** section at the top of the box, type in the appropriate number of pixels for **Width** or **Height.** If you haven't been told what pixel dimensions to use, limiting the Width to no more than 580 pixels and the Height to no more than 400 pixels will make a file that will display the entire image, even on a small screen.

The "Resample Image" option must be turned ON in order to make it possible to change the Pixel Dimensions.

Sharpening. Changing the dimensions of a file with "Resample Image" turned ON can cause the image to look slightly fuzzy. ◉ *The tip at the left tells why resampling can soften an image.*

To bring back some of the original detail, you can use the Unsharp Mask filter: **Choose Filter > Sharpen > Unsharp Mask** to open the filter's dialog box. When the Unsharp Mask dialog box opens, **experiment with the settings.** Unsharp Mask looks for "edges" in the image. For each edge, it accentuates the contrast between the color on one side and the color on the other. This makes the edges more distinct, and thus the whole image looks sharper.

In the Unsharp Mask dialog box, you may want to start with Amount set at 50%, Radius at 1 pixel, and Threshold at 0 levels, and then increase the Amount if needed to get the degree of sharpening you want.

Saving the file. Save the file (**File > Save As**) in **JPEG** format. Clicking the "Save" button opens the JPEG Options dialog box:

If your main goal is small file size, try starting with a setting of 3, with "Baseline Optimized" checked. Then work your way up to higher quality until you reach the biggest file size you're willing to accept. (Make sure "Preview" is turned on so you can watch the changes.)

Instead of using File > Save As, you can optimize the image (reduce the file size as small as possible without losing too much image quality) by using **File > Save For Web.** (To learn about using Save For Web, **choose Help > Photoshop Help, click on "Search," type** "Optimizing images" in the entry box, and **click the "Search" button.**

A LAYER STYLE TUTORIAL

In this tutorial you'll learn how to:

1 Set up Photoshop to work with Styles

2 Apply Styles

3 Alter a Style

4 Copy and paste a Style

5 Convert a Background so you can apply a Style

6 Replace a Style

7 Scale a Style

8 Save a library of Style presets

9 Change layer content but keep the Style

10 Add a Rollover Style in Image-Ready

1 Preparing the file. Make sure the **One-Click Wow! Styles** are inside Photoshop 7's Styles folder. 👁 *See "One-Click Wow! Quick Start" on page 3 for directions for installing Styles.*

Start Photoshop and make sure the Layers palette is open (if not, **choose Window > Show Layers**). Open the Styles palette in the same way (**choose Window > Show Styles**). Click the little triangle in the top right corner of the Styles palette and choose Large List.

For each Style, the Styles palette's Large List view shows a thumbnail plus the Style's full name. The bottom section of the pop-out menu lists all the Styles libraries in Photoshop's Styles folder.

Now use the Styles palette's pop-out menu again to **load Wow 7-15 Organic Styles** from the libraries at the bottom of the menu; in the "caution" box that appears, **click the "Append" button** to *add* this library to your currently loaded Styles, **or click "OK"** to *replace* them. 👁 *See the tip on page 23 about appending versus replacing.* Then **append the Wow 7-03 Tint FX Styles and the Wow 7-17 Stroke Styles.**

Click "Append" to add to the current Styles in the Styles palette; click "OK" to replace them.

Next, copy the **Wow-Styles Tutorial 1.psd** file from the **Wow-Styles Tutorial** folder on the **One-Click Wow!** CD-ROM onto your hard disk drive. Then open this file (**choose File > Open**).

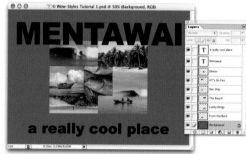

*The **Wow-Styles Tutorial 1.psd** file*

With the Layers palette open, you can see that the **Wow-Styles Tutorial 1.psd** file, which is a postcard layout, has each of its components on a separate layer:

- Type, in the Arial Black font, has been set in two separate layers so different Styles can be applied to the two settings.

- The photos are all on separate layers also, but they have all been *linked,* by clicking on one layer's name in the Layers palette and then clicking in the "links" column to the left of the thumbnail for each of the other photos. This allows all the photos to be moved or "styled" together.

- At the bottom of the stack of layers is a gray-filled *Background.*

None of the layers in this file has a Style applied to it yet.

2 Applying Layer Styles. With each element on a layer of its own, you'll be able to add color and dimension by applying different Styles to the individual layers:

- For the "Mentawai" type layer, in the Styles palette click **Wow-Organics 05**, a dimen-

▶ *When you apply a Style to a layer, the 🅘 icon appears to the right of the name in the Layers palette. Also, indented under the layer's name is a list of the individual effects that make up the Style. You can click on the "eye" icon next to any effect to temporarily turn off the effect. Click in this column again to toggle the effect back on. To make the Layers palette more compact, you can also click the tiny triangle to the left of the 🅘 to hide the list of effects; clicking again expands the list.*

▶ *When you open a library of Styles, you have the choice of appending (adding) the new Styles to the ones that are already in the Styles palette, or replacing the current Styles with the new ones. Each choice has advantages and disadvantages. Appending can lead to a very long list that can tie up RAM and also make it hard to find a particular Style. On the other hand, if you replace the current set of Styles rather than adding on, you risk losing any Styles that you've created, imported, or modified and added to the list but haven't yet saved as part of a library.*

sional Style that includes shadows, glows, a photographic Pattern Overlay (the weave), and a tint created by a Color Overlay.

- For "a really cool place" use **Wow-Stroke 01**, made with three Overlays: Color, Gradient, and Pattern.

- For the central ("Dinner") photo layer, use **Wow-Tint FX 01**, a "partial sepiatone" Style made with a white inner glow, a dark drop shadow, and a color overlay that partially replaces color with brown tones.

*The **Wow-Styles Tutorial 1.psd** file after Styles have been applied to the two type layers and the "Dinner" photo layer. In the Layers palette, small 🅘 icons mark the "styled" layers.*

3 Customizing a Style. It's easy to modify a Style once you've applied it. To change the Style for the "Dinner" photo layer, **double-click the 🅘 icon** next to its name in the Layers palette to open the Layer Styles dialog box. Then **click "Inner Glow"** in the list on the left side of the box to see the settings.

*The built-in Size setting for the Inner Glow in the **Wow-Tint FX 01** Style is 32 px (pixels).*

Reduce the Inner Glow's Size setting to 10 px (pixels) to shrink the edge effect. **Click "OK"** to close the dialog box.

Before (left) and after reducing the Inner Glow's Size setting to 10 px

4 Copying and pasting a Style. To apply this modified Style to the other photo layers, **copy and paste it, as follows: Right-click** (Windows) or **Ctrl-click** (Mac) **the 🅘 icon for the "Dinner" layer,** and when the context-sensitive menu appears, **choose Copy Layer Style.** Then, since the other photos are already linked, simply **right/Ctrl-click the 🅘 icon for any other photo layer** and **choose Paste Layer Style To Linked,** and all the photos will share the same Style. (For pasting a Style to a *single layer,* the choice would be Paste Layer Style.)

Copying the Style (left) and pasting it to the other linked photo layers (right)

continued on page 24

A LAYER STYLE TUTORIAL

continued

▶ *In Photoshop 7, double-clicking the **name** of the layer selects the name itself so you can edit it to rename the layer.*

*But double-clicking **the image thumbnail** or **the ✱ icon** will open the Layer Style dialog box so you can customize a Style that has been applied to the layer.*

*The **Wow-Styles Tutorial 1.psd** file after the **Wow-Tint FX 01** Style has been pasted to the linked layers*

5 Converting a *Background*. To make an "instant background," you can use a **One-Click Wow!** Style to fill an entire layer with a pattern that consists of an image or texture. But to replace the gray background of the **Wow-Styles Tutorial 1.psd** file you're working on, you first have to turn the *Background* into a layer that can accept a Style. To do this, **double-click the *Background's* thumbnail in the Layers palette**, type a new layer name in the New Layer dialog box if you like (such as "Base Layer"), and **click "OK."**

Converting the Background

To turn the "Base Layer" into bamboo, click **Wow-Organics 16** in the Styles palette.

*The file after the **Wow-Organics 16** Style has been applied to the bottom layer (The **Wow-Styles Tutorial 2.psd** file shows the project at this stage.)*

6 Replacing Styles. One of the great advantages of Layer Styles is that you can change the entire "look and feel" of a Photoshop composition instantly, simply by replacing some of the Layer Styles. To target the layer whose Style you want to change, click its name in the Layers palette. Then load the appropriate **One-Click Wow! Styles** library into the Styles palette (as in step 1) and click on a new Style. For instance:

- To change the Style for the "Base Layer," load **Wow 7-14 Rock Styles** and choose **Wow-Rocks 20,** a complex sandstone-like texture.

- For the "Mentawai" type, **load Wow 7-09 Metal Styles** and **apply Wow-Metals 06,** a golden metallic treatment that includes a Pattern Overlay and a matching Texture.

*On the "Mentawai" type and the "Base Layer," new Styles (**Wow-Metals 06** and **Wow-Rock 20,** respectively) have replaced the old ones.*

7 Scaling a Style. Scaling often helps to "custom-fit" a Style to a specific graphic. In the Layers palette, **click "a really cool place"** to target this layer. Then **right-click** (Windows) or **Ctrl-click** (Mac) the ✱ icon to the right of the layer's name and **choose Scale Effects** from the context-sensitive menu. In the Scale Layer Effects dialog box, **click the little triangle** to the right of the "100" to pop out the slider. Then **move the slider to the left** to scale the pattern and reduce the offset of the

► *If you want to create a library of Styles that includes some or all of the ones currently in the Styles palette,* **choose Edit > Preset Manager** *and* **choose Styles** *from the pop-out Preset Type menu to display the current Styles. Then Shift-click the Styles that you want to include, and click the "Save Set" button.*

Clicking "Save Set" to create a library from the selected Styles

When the Save dialog box appears, name your new library, navigate to the Styles folder (inside Photoshop 7's Presets folder) and click the "Save" button.

Saving the new library into the Styles folder so it will automatically appear in the Styles palette's pop-out menu

drop shadow. Moving the shadow makes the lettering seem closer to the background.

Before (top left) and after reducing the Scale to 20%

8 Saving a library of Styles. When you alter a Style you've applied, such as the modified partial sepiatone made in step 3 or the scaled Style in step 7), it's a good idea to give the new Style its own name and save it as part of a Styles library. That way, you can choose it directly from the Styles palette in the future. Saving a custom Style is a two-step process:

• First you add the Style to the list of Styles currently displayed in the Styles palette: **Target the layer that has the Style** you want to save (such as the "Dinner" layer), then **click the "Create new style" button** at the bottom of the Styles palette. In the New Style dialog box, leave the check boxes set as they are, **name the Style,** and **click "OK."**

With the "styled" layer targeted, clicking the "Create new style" button starts the process of saving the current Style. When you close the New Style box, your Style will appear in the last position in the Styles palette.

• Then to protect your new Style from being lost if you replace the current Styles, **choose Edit > Preset Manager** and **choose Styles** from the Preset Type menu in the Preset Manager dialog box. Now you can create a new library that includes any or all of the currently loaded Styles. ◉ *See the tip at the left for directions on saving a new library of Styles.* When you've finished saving libraries, **click the "Done" button.**

9 Changing layer content. Part of the magic of Layer Styles is that they "stick with" the layer. So if you change the content of a layer to which a Style has been applied, the Style instantly conforms to the new content:

• To change the font in the "Mentawai" layer, **target this layer** in the Layers palette, then **choose the Type tool and choose a new font** from the pop-up list in the Options bar. (If you want to change the font for the entire layer, as we do here, there's no need to select any text with the cursor.)

Before (top) and after changing the font (If you don't have the CCDutchCourage font, use another font of your choice.)

• To change the wording in the "a really cool place" layer, **target this layer, drag the Type tool cursor over the type** to select it, **press the Caps Lock key,** and **type** "BEYOND

A LAYER STYLE TUTORIAL
continued

▶ *The Styles palettes in Photoshop and ImageReady are similar, but not exactly the same. For instance:*

- *Loading a library of Styles in one program doesn't automatically load it in the other program. You have to load the two programs' Styles palettes separately.*

- *Unlike Photoshop, Image-Ready doesn't have a Large List option for the styles palette display. So the Small List option is best for seeing both a "swatch" of each Style and the Style's full name.*

▶ *Since there is no Preset Manager in ImageReady, to save a library of Styles, target an empty layer so you won't make changes to your file, then delete any unwanted Styles one-by-one by selecting them in the Styles palette and clicking the "Delete style" button (the trash can) at the bottom of the palette. When you've eliminated all the Styles you don't want, click the small triangle in the upper right corner of the Styles palette and choose Save Styles from the pop-out menu.*

THE DREAM"; **press the Enter key** to finalize the change.

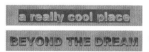

The selected type

After editing the type

To complete the Photoshop part of this tutorial, change the font for the "BEYOND THE DREAM" layer. **Wow-Styles Tutorial 3.psd** shows the file at this stage.

10 Adding a Rollover Style in Image-Ready. In ImageReady 7 you can use all the Styles you can use in Photoshop 7. And you can also take advantage of *Rollover Styles*, which have built-in interactivity.

Start up ImageReady 7 and open the **Wow-Styles Tutorial 4.psd** file. This file is a version of the postcard file, scaled down for the Web and with button graphics added. Each oval button is on its own layer.

*The **Wow-Style Tutorial 4.psd** file*

From the pop-out menu of ImageReady 7's Styles palette, choose the **Wow 7-20 Button Styles** and **click the "Append" or "Replace" button.** ⊙ *See the tip on page 23 about choosing to append or replace Styles.*

Next, in the Layers palette, **click the name of one of the button Shape layers** to target this layer, and **in the Styles palette click the Wow Button 24-All Three** Style. ImageReady will apply the Style and create an interactive

slice (the smallest area that includes the entire button graphic and its Style elements).

*Before (top) and after applying the **Wow Button 24-All Three** Rollover Style to one of the button layers*

Apply the same Rollover Style to the other button graphics.

*The **Wow-Styles Tutorial 4.psd** file with the **Wow Button 24-All Three** Rollover Style applied to all the buttons*

As in Photoshop, you can make changes to a "styled" button: **Target a button layer, press Ctrl/⌘-T** (for Edit > Free Transform), and **Alt/Option-drag inward on a side handle** of the Transform box. (Linked buttons will be transformed together.)

When you transform a "Rollover-styled" button, the Style and its layer-based slice will both conform to the new shape. Press the Enter key to complete the transformation.

2 Styles for Photos

In this section you'll find **One-Click Wow Styles** designed especially to enhance photos. Some of these Styles are also ideal for paintings you create using the methods described in "Section 4."

▶ *It's likely that many of the photo files that you'll want to apply a Style to will need one of the changes below:*

• *If the image is a "flattened" file — that is, it consists only of a Photoshop "Background" layer — you'll want to double-click on its name to change it to a non-Background so it can accept a Style.*

• *Many of the **Wow Styles** for photos create edge treatments, such as dimensional frames. Some of the effects that are built into these Styles — for instance, Drop Shadows — are designed to extend outward from the edges of the image. For these effects to show up, you'll need extra space around the edges. To add space, choose Image > Canvas Size and increase the Width and Height.*

• *Many digital photos and scanned images are stored in the compressed JPEG format. Opening and then resaving these files as JPEGs again can create an obvious reduction in photo quality. So after you edit a JPEG — by applying a Style or any other way — be sure to save it in a different (lossless) format such as the native Photoshop (.psd) format. ◉ See the tip on page 20 for a discussion of file formats available in Photoshop.*

PHOTO GALLERY

On these next four pages are just a few samples of what you can do with the seven libraries of **Wow 7 Styles designed for photos.** (Pages 32–45 show examples of all of the Styles in these libraries.) For some of the images shown here, the Styles have been scaled to fit. 👁 *See "Scaling a Style" on pages 10–11 for tips on scaling.*

1 **Color FX 07** *"colorizes" the photo, with the colors depending on the image.* **2** **Edges 01** *creates a vignette for use on a white background.* **3** **Frame 04** *is used here with its mat color changed, as described on page 34.* **4** **Edges 08's** *negative edges conform to the content of the photo.* **5** **Tint FX 03** *is a "75% sepiatone"; it applies a brown tint but keeps some of the original color (compare examples 18 and 19 on page 31).* **6** *Framing several photos with the same Style (here* **Frame 07***) helps unify them as a group.* **7** **Darkroom 09** *adds drama to clouds and sunsets by overlaying a red-to-yellow gradient.* **8** *Used on this color photo,* **Edges 08** *inverts the color to form a custom edge.* **9** **Tint FX 06** *creates a textured blue duotone effect with a soft inner edge and outer shadow.*

continued on page 30

1

2

3

4

5

6

7

8

9

10

PHOTO GALLERY
continued

10 Here ***Darkroom 04***'s exaggerated color makes a lively image even more so. **11** ***Edges 03***'s soft, dark edges, combined with the round-cornered framing, enhance the antique character of this photo. **12** ***Frame 05***'s dark beveled wood also adds to the antique look of this photo. **13** The lightly etched border of ***Frame 09*** lends the modern look of a slip-in glass frame. **14** ***Frame 06*** creates the "retro" look of tortoiseshell Bakelite. **15** ***Texture 04*** overlays a canvas-and-brush-stroke pattern. **16** The dark semi-transparent border in ***Edges 05*** provides a modern framing treatment. **17** Here ***Darkroom 04*** builds color (compare the exaggerated effect in 10). **18** ***Tint FX 01*** overlays a 60% sepiatone on the original color and adds both a glow and a shadow to the edges. **19** ***Tint FX 09***'s sepia completely replaces the original color and also adds a canvas texture. **20** ***Edges 07*** puts the photo under clear, polished acrylic. **21** The stippled transparent borders of ***Edges 04*** allow whatever is on the layers below to show through. **22** ***Frame 03***'s beveled molding comes with a beige mat inside the frame. (The mats for all of the ***Wow 7-02 Frame Styles*** can be turned on or off by setting the Inner Glow's Opacity to 100% or 0%; you can also change the Inner Glow's Size to control mat width.)

11

12

13

15

14

16

17

18

19

20

21

22

Edges

The **Wow-Edges** Layer Styles create vignettes and border treatments for photos. **Edges 06–10** include drop shadows. *See the tips on page 34 to learn how to convert a Background so you can apply a Style, and how to add space so the drop shadow can show.*

Edges 01 creates a soft-edged vignette for a photo that will be placed on a white background. **Edges 02** desaturates and lightens the edges. **Edges 03** darkens the border. **Edges 04** dithers to transparency, so it creates a "speckled vignette" that lets the background show through regardless of its color.

Edges 05 and **06** provide two speckled framing treatments.

The highlights at the edges of **07** create the look of an image under acrylic resin. This Style can be useful as a button treatment for a photo or an icon.

In **08–10** the shape and colors of the border area will vary, depending on the photo you apply it to, because these Styles invert the colors at the edges of the image. If you turn off visibility for the drop shadow for **10,** it provides another "vignette to white" option.

ORIGINAL PHOTO: © CORBIS IMAGES ROYALTY FREE, COUPLES

Wow-Edges 01

Wow-Edges 02

Wow-Edges 03

Wow-Edges 04

Wow-Edges 05

Wow-Edges 06

Wow-Edges 07

Wow-Edges 08

Wow-Edges 09

Wow-Edges 10

Frames

With one click, each of the Wow-Frame Layer Styles creates a dimensional picture-frame treatment.

▶ *If you try to apply a Style to a Background layer, nothing will happen. To convert a Background to a non-Background layer that can accept a style, double-click "Background" in the Layers palette and then click OK.*

If you want to include the drop shadow that's built into these **Wow-Frame** Styles, there has to be some empty, transparent space around the image for the shadow to extend into.

▶ *To add empty space at the edges, choose Image > Canvas Size and increase the Width and Height.*

Each Style in the **Wow-Frame** set includes a "color mat" Option. Once you've applied the Style to a layer, if the mat isn't visible, you can make it appear as follows: Double-click the ⓕ icon next to the layer's name in the Layers palette and when the Layer Styles dialog box opens, click "Inner Glow" in the list along the left edge; then in the Inner Glow section, change the Opacity to 100%. (You can also do the opposite — completely "turn off" a mat by setting the Opacity to 0%.) To change a mat's color, click the Inner Glow's color swatch and pick a new color.

Frame 07 and **08** are made of woven materials. **Frame 09** sandwiches an image between sheets of glass.
👁 *See the "Photo Gallery" on pages 28–31 for more description of individual* **Wow-Frame** *Styles.*

ORIGINAL PHOTO: © JHDAVIS DESIGN

Wow-Frame 01*

Wow-Frame 02*

Wow-Frame 03*

Wow-Frame 04*

All of the **Wow-Frame Styles include surface patterns or textures. If you need to scale one of these Styles to fit your file, there are certain scaling percentages that will ensure that the patterns stay sharp and clear.* 👁 *See "Scaling a Style" on pages 10–11 for help.*

Wow-Frame 05*

Wow-Frame 06*

Wow-Frame 07*

Wow-Frame 08*

Wow-Frame 09*

Wow-Frame 10*

Tints & Antique Effects

The **Wow-Tint FX** Styles create sepiatone (**01–04**), black-and-white (**05**), blue tint (**06** and **07**) and antique effects (**08–10**), keeping different amounts of the original color. (Styles **02**, **05**, **08**, and **09** replace the original color entirely.)

All the **Wow-Tint FX** Styles except **05** include drop shadows. ◉ *See "Frames" on page 34 to learn how to add space so the drop shadow will show up.*

You can use any of the **Tint FX** series *without* the lightened or darkened edges. First apply the Style, then double-click the *f* to the right of the layer's name in the Layers palette, click "Inner Glow" in the list of effects in the Layer Style dialog box, and in the Inner Glow section move the Size slider left to 0.

Tint FX 08 "antiques" an image by adding a dark edge, a slightly tinted black-and-white tone, and a "pebbled" surface. **Tint FX 09** is similar, but with a light edge and a canvas texture, and **10** has a subtler edge and a 5% contribution of the original color of the image. You can make the texture less pro-

nounced by reducing the Depth in the Texture section, listed under "Bevel and Emboss" in the Layer Style dialog box, or by reducing the Opacity of the Pattern Overlay.

Wow-Tint FX 01

Wow-Tint FX 02

Wow-Tint FX 03

Wow-Tint FX 04

Wow-Tint FX 05

Wow-Tint FX 06

Wow-Tint FX 07

Wow-Tint FX 08*

Wow-Tint FX 09*

Wow-Tint FX 10*

*Some of the **Wow-Tint FX** Styles include patterns or textures. If you need to scale one of these Styles to fit your file, there are certain scaling percentages that will ensure that the patterns stay sharp and clear. 👁 See "Scaling a Style" on pages 10–11 for help.*

Color Overlay Effects

The **Wow-Color FX** Styles use overlays of color — either solid colors or gradients — to create multicolor tints, changing the color of an image for practical or surreal and dramatic effects.

Styles **01** and **02** darken and lighten the image, respectively, so that the image can serve as a subtle background for light or dark type set in a layer above it.

Styles **03–07** create posterization and color-inversion special effects based on the colors in the original image.

The gradient overlays in **08–10** replace the color in the original image with multiple hues.

▶ *After you apply a **Wow-Color FX** Style to a layer, you can change the colors themselves or the angle or position of the color blend as follows: Double-click the ⓕ to the right of the "styled" layer's name in the Layers palette. In the Layer Style dialog box, click on the "Color Overlay" or "Gradient Overlay" entry in the list at the left side of the dialog box. Then reduce the Opacity to reduce the Overlay's contribution. Or for a Gradient Overlay choose a different color combination from the pop-out Gradient palette. Change the direction of the color change by dragging in the Angle circle; or drag in the main working window to reposition the gradient with respect to the image.*

Wow-Color FX 01

Wow-Color FX 02

Wow-Color FX 03

Wow-Color FX 04

Wow-Color FX 05

Wow-Color FX 06

Wow-Color FX 07

Wow-Color FX 08

Wow-Color FX 09

Wow-Color FX 10

Darkroom & Image-Enhancing Effects

Wow-Darkroom Styles **01–03** focus attention and add subtle enhancements; **01** darkens the top and bottom, **02** darkens the top only, and **03** darkens the edges and lightens the center.*

Style **04** exaggerates the saturation (or intensity) of the colors. (It will have no effect on a black-and-white picture.)

Style **05** adds a dark edging and also *solarizes* the image, turning some colors negative and leaving others positive. To use the effect without the darkened edges, you can apply the Style, then double-click "Inner Glow" in the list of effects that appears in the Layers palette, and move the Inner Glow's Size slider to 0.

Style **06** makes a negative. And **07** converts the image to a limited range of colors; light colors turn yellow and orange, darker colors become gray.

Styles **08–10** are particularly good for enhancing sunset skies; you can move the gradients to position the colors relative to the horizon. ◉ *See the tip on page 38 for realigning a gradient.*

See the tip on page 38 for realigning a gradient.

ORIGINAL PHOTOS: © JHDAVIS DESIGN

Wow-Darkroom 01   **Wow-Darkroom 02**

Wow-Darkroom 03   **Wow-Darkroom 04**

**Wow-Darkroom 11–15 are subtle variations on Wow-Darkroom 03.*

Wow-Darkroom 05

Wow-Darkroom 06

Wow-Darkroom 07

Wow-Darkroom 08

Wow-Darkroom 09

Wow-Darkroom 10

Film Grain, Noise & Mezzotints

A pattern or texture can provide a subtle artistic treatment for a single image, or it can help to unify several photos. 👁 *See the tip on page 34 to learn how to convert a Background so you can apply a Style.*

Some of the Styles in the **Wow-Grain** set produce mezzotint-like effects, adding dots, lines, or streaks. Others (**01–03**) can simulate film grain or "digital noise." These can help hide pixel artifacts that may appear in low-resolution images or help unify photos in different layers of a collage. You can customize a **Wow-Grain** Style after you apply it by double-clicking the *ƒ* that appears to the right of the "styled" layer's name in the Layers palette, then clicking the "Pattern Overlay" entry in the list in the Layer Style dialog box. You can then Scale the grain to the size you need, or change its Opacity, or change the Blend mode — for instance, switching the Blend mode from Overlay to Soft Light will reduce the contrast of the grain.

Styles **04–06** are variations on a reticulated mezzotint effect, and **07** and **08** create irregular blotches for a freckled or dappled look.

Style **09** creates a diagonal pattern of brushed lines. And **10** creates a horizontal pattern of high-tech scan lines.

ORIGINAL PHOTO: © CORBIS IMAGES ROYALTY FREE, FOOD PERSPECTIVES

Wow-Grain 01*

Wow-Grain 02*

Wow-Grain 03*

Wow-Grain 04*

The names of all Styles in the **Wow-Grain library include the * symbol, which indicates that a surface pattern or texture is part of the Style. If you need to scale one of these Styles to fit your file, there are certain scaling percentages that will ensure that the patterns stay sharp and clear.* 👁 *See "Scaling a Style" on pages 10–11 for help.*

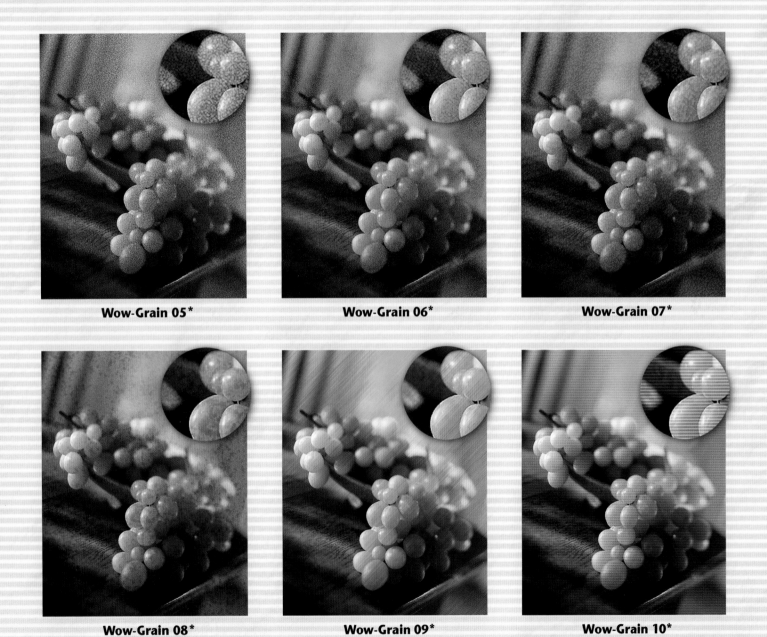

Wow-Grain 05*

Wow-Grain 06*

Wow-Grain 07*

Wow-Grain 08*

Wow-Grain 09*

Wow-Grain 10*

Paper, Canvas & Other Texture Overlays

When you create a painting in Photoshop — whether "from scratch" or from a photo — adding the texture of paper or canvas can complete the illusion. The **Wow! Textures** can also simply be applied to a photo or graphic to add personality. 👁 *See the tip on page 34 to learn how to convert a Background so you can apply a Style.*

Wow-Texture 01 simulates watercolor paper. Style **02** is an irregularly textured canvas, **03** "bevels" any semitransparent brush strokes you apply and adds a canvas texture as well, and **04** simulates canvas with impasto brush strokes. Style **05** simulates pebble board, **06** and **07** are rough surfaces for pastel or chalk, **08** is cracked paint, **09** simulates watercolor with salt stains, and **10** simulates the fresco effect of painting on a plastered surface.

The "painting" used in this example (a detail of which is shown below) was made from a photo by using Tool Presets from the **Wow-AH-Pastels** library, which are based on the Art History brush. 👁 *See "Media Brushes" on page 79 to find out how to use the Wow-Textures in combination with the Wow Tool Presets.*

Wow-Texture 01*

Wow-Texture 02*

Wow-Texture 03*

Wow-Texture 04*

*All of the **Wow-Texture** Styles include surface patterns or textures. If you need to scale one of these Styles to fit your file, there are certain scaling percentages that will ensure that the patterns stay sharp and clear. 👁 "Scaling a Style" on pages 10–11 tells how.*

Wow-Texture 05*

Wow-Texture 06*

Wow-Texture 07*

Wow-Texture 08*

Wow-Texture 09*

Wow-Texture 10*

3 Styles for Type & Graphics

The Styles in this section (from **Wow 7** libraries **08–20**) were designed to add color, dimension, and material characteristics to type and graphics. Choose a Style for your project, apply it, and then tweak it if you like, as described in "Customizing Styles" on pages 12–13.

▶ *You can "combine" Styles by applying separate Styles to the layered elements of a graphic. For instance, to create the look of a carved, translucent amulet, the* **Wow-Gems 19** *Style was applied to a graphic on the upper layer, and the lighter* **Wow-Gems 08** *was applied to an oval shape on the layer below.*

When you arrive at a combination of Styles you like and you think you might want to use it again, one way to save the "combined Style" is to save (in Photoshop format) a file you've applied it to. Whenever you want to use the combination again, open this file and copy and paste the Styles, as described in "Copying & Pasting Styles" on page 14. 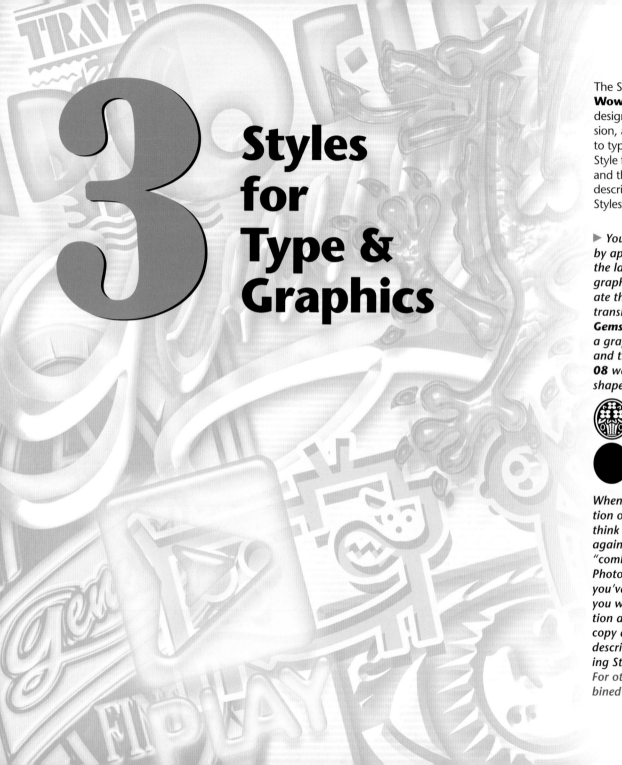 *For other examples of "combined" Styles, see page 50.*

TYPE & GRAPHICS GALLERY

The next five pages show some of the "magic" you can work on graphics and type using the 12 sets of Wow Styles on pages 52–75. (Some Styles have been scaled to fit the graphics shown here.)

1, 2, 3 *Rocks 03, 04,* and *05 are three different color versions of the same rough rock.*
4 *Rocks 12 is white stone.*
5 *The thick gold stroke of* **Stroke 09,** *which extends outward from all the edges of this black graphic, fills in the small negative spaces, leaving transparency only in the large sun element at the bottom.* **6** *Chrome 17 applies a dark finish with bright, raised bevels at the edges.*
7 *After* **Plastic 19** *was applied, the rainbow Gradient Overlay was repositioned to put its colors where we wanted them.*
8 *The* **Rocks 02** *Style was scaled to 25% after it was applied.* **9** *Glass 19 makes the flat shapes and lettering of this type look like water.* **10** *Like many of the other Wow Styles designed for photos,* **Edges 05** *can work well on graphics also.*

TYPE & GRAPHICS GALLERY
continued

11 *Woods 06* adds dimension and the grain and glow of smooth polished wood.

12 *Halo 13* lightens the interior, adding an overall speckle and a dark outer "halo"; like most Styles with interior edge effects, it looks different on bolder elements than on thin ones. **13** *Metals 19* simulates chiseled steel. **14** *Glow 03* and *04* turn edges into glowing neon tubes. **15** *Stroke 06* and *07* add color strokes and fills; sharp shadows add dimension.

16 *Rocks 01* creates bricks, complete with indented mortar. **17** *Gems 19* on the graphics and the lighter *Gems 08* on the oval in the layer below combine for a backlit effect. **18** *Plastic 15* creates an opaque, polished surface.

19 *Metals 15* adds the look of rusted, deeply pitted metal. **20** *Plastic 09* produces a rounded, translucent blue-green. **21** *Stroke 20* is great for "comic book" type. **22** In the **Chrome** set, *15* is darkest. **23** *Glass 20* produces rounded smoked glass. **24** *Organics 19* produces a rustic woven look. **25** *Halo 09* "carves" into the surface of the layers below.

continued on page 50

17

18

19

TOXIC

20

BEND O FLEX

21 *"Gee whiz!"*

22

23

24

 25

TYPE & GRAPHICS GALLERY
continued

26 *Glow 10* turns the lines of this logo into neon tubes in the "off" state. **27** *Glow 08* turns the neon "on." **28** *Rocks 07* is raw Kryptonite. **29** *Plastic 05* creates swirled color inside chrome edges. **30** *Woods 18* produces beveled pine. **31** Gradient-filled *Stroke 18* applied to a rectangle makes a surface for *Halo 11,* applied to a graphic in the layer above, to "carve" into. **32** *Plastic 13* applied to a layer above a shape treated with *Plastic 14* creates a stamped sign. **33** The bright placer gold of *Metals 16* on the star complements the duller bronze of *Metals 15* on the type. **34** *Metals 09* produces brushed steel with polished edges. **35** *Halo 16* adds a rainbow halo without changing the graphic's original color, here red. **36** *Organics 04* makes a raised green edge around a woven fill. **37** *Halo 18* makes the art disappear, leaving only a dark exterior halo. **38** *Gems 11* produces a raised abalone texture. **39** *Chrome 13* adds a matte finish to broad, flat areas. **40** *Plastic 08* is a clear, rounded blue. **41** The boldness of each part of the graphic determines how much of *Glow 16*'s yellow inner glow can color the interior.

26

35

36

34

HAPPY ANNIVERSARY!

37

38

39

40

PLAY

41

Chromes

The Layer Styles in the **Wow-Chrome** set were designed for use on type or graphics, to simulate various kinds of reflective surfaces. The Styles are shown here applied to a file with a Resolution setting of 225 pixels/inch.

Wow-Chrome 11 is the only one of these Layer Styles that allows some of the original color of the graphic or type to come through in the chrome. So if you had started with a green symbol, for instance, instead of the gray shown here, your chrome would show a slight green tint. All other **Wow-Chrome** Styles produce the same results regardless of the starting color. 👁 *See "One-Click Wow! Quick Start" on pages 3–5 for directions for loading Styles*

*In Styles whose names include the * symbol, a built-in surface pattern or texture is used to create the illusion of the environment reflected in the chrome. If you need to scale one of these Styles to fit your file, there are certain scaling percentages that will ensure that the patterns stay sharp and clear. 👁 See "Scaling a Style" on pages 10–11 for help.

Original Graphic

Wow-Chrome 01*

Wow-Chrome 02*

Wow-Chrome 03

Wow-Chrome 04

Wow-Chrome 05

Wow-Chrome 06

Wow-Chrome 07

Wow-Chrome 08

Wow-Chrome 09

Wow-Chrome 10*

Wow-Chrome 11*

Wow-Chrome 12*

Wow-Chrome 13

Wow-Chrome 14*

Wow-Chrome 15

Wow-Chrome 16*

Wow-Chrome 17*

Wow-Chrome 18

Wow-Chrome 19

Wow-Chrome 20

Metals

The Layer Styles in the **Wow-Metals** set were designed to make type or graphics look like they were stamped, chiseled, molded, or otherwise created from gold, steel, iron, or other metals, some glowing hot. Rough-surfaced Styles typically use the same pattern both in a Pattern Overlay effect and in the Texture aspect of the Bevel And Emboss effect. The results shown here were achieved by applying each of the Styles to a file with a Resolution setting of 225 pixels/inch.

👁 *See "One-Click Wow! Quick Start," pages 3–5 for directions for loading Styles.*
👁 *See "Scaling a Style," pages 10–11 to learn about the relationship between Layer Styles and the Resolution setting in the Image Size dialog box.*

* Styles whose names include the * symbol have a built-in surface pattern or texture. If you need to scale one of these Styles to fit your file, there are certain scaling percentages that will ensure that the patterns stay sharp and clear.
👁 *See "Scaling a Style," pages 10–11.*

Original Graphic

Wow-Metals 01*

Wow-Metals 02*

Wow-Metals 03*

Wow-Metals 04*

Wow-Metals 05*

Wow-Metals 06*

Wow-Metals 07*

Wow-Metals 08*

Wow-Metals 09*

Wow-Metals 10*

Wow-Metals 11*

Wow-Metals 12*

Wow-Metals 13*

Wow-Metals 14*

Wow-Metals 15*

Wow-Metals 16*

Wow-Metals 17

Wow-Metals 18

Wow-Metals 19*

Wow-Metals 20

Glass, Ice & Crystal

The Layer Styles in the **Wow-Glass** set were designed to make type or graphics look as if they were formed of transparent crystalline materials. Some of them also feature highly reflective textured surfaces.

The **Wow-Glass** Styles completely remove or replace the original color of the graphic, so that no matter what color it was to start with, the original color is not evident in the "styled" element.

The effects shown here are the results of applying the **Wow-Glass** Styles to a file with a Resolution setting of 225 pixels/inch. 👁 *See "Scaling a Style" on pages 10–11 to learn about the relationship between Layer Styles and the Resolution setting.*

*Styles whose names include the * symbol have a built-in surface pattern or texture. If you need to scale one of these Styles to fit your file, there are certain scaling percentages that will ensure that the patterns stay sharp and clear.* 👁 *See "Scaling a Style," pages 10–11.*

Original Graphic **Wow-Glass 01** **Wow-Glass 02**

Wow-Glass 03* **Wow-Glass 04** **Wow-Glass 05***

Wow-Glass 06 **Wow-Glass 07** **Wow-Glass 08**

Wow-Glass 09

Wow-Glass 10*

Wow-Glass 11

Wow-Glass 12

Wow-Glass 13*

Wow-Glass 14*

Wow-Glass 15

Wow-Glass 16

Wow-Glass 17

Wow-Glass 18*

Wow-Glass 19

Wow-Glass 20*

Gems & Smooth Stones

The Layer Styles in the **Wow-Gems** set were designed to endow type or graphics with the colorful brilliance of polished gems, amber, or shells, as well as marble and other kinds of stone, with accompanying translucency and reflectivity.

All of the **Wow-Gems** Styles apply surface patterning, and one (**Wow-Gems 11**) has a bumpy surface texture as well.

The effects shown here are the results of applying the **Wow-Gems** Styles to a file with a Resolution setting of 225 pixels/inch. ◉ *See "Scaling a Style" on pages 10–11 for the relationship between Layer Styles and the Resolution setting.*

The names of all the Styles in the **Wow-Gems set include the * symbol, which indicates that a surface pattern or texture is part of the Style. If you need to scale one of these Styles to fit your file, there are certain scaling percentages that will ensure that the patterns stay sharp and clear. ◉ See "Scaling a Style" on pages 10–11.*

Original Graphic   Wow-Gems 01*   Wow-Gems 02*

Wow-Gems 03*   Wow-Gems 04*   Wow-Gems 05*

Wow-Gems 06*   Wow-Gems 07*   Wow-Gems 08*

Wow-Gems 09*

Wow-Gems 10*

Wow-Gems 11*

Wow-Gems 12*

Wow-Gems 13*

Wow-Gems 14*

Wow-Gems 15*

Wow-Gems 16*

Wow-Gems 17*

Wow-Gems 18*

Wow-Gems 19*

Wow-Gems 20*

Plastics

The Styles in the **Wow-Plastics** set imitate various kinds of plastics, some opaque and others translucent. The colors are integrated into the Styles, so the original color of the type or graphic doesn't affect the final result. Most of the **Wow-Plastics** are smooth-surfaced, but four (**03**, **13**, **14** and **18**) are textured.

Wow-Plastics 13 and **14** are designed to work together to create the look of a sign or license plate — the black is applied to a layer with graphics or type, and the yellow is applied to the larger shape of the sign or plate in the layer underneath. 👁 *See "Type & Graphics Gallery" on page 50 for a layered sign example.*

The effects shown here are the results of applying the Styles to a file with a Resolution of 225 pixels/inch.

*Styles whose names include the * symbol have a built-in surface pattern or texture. If you need to scale one of these Styles to fit your file, there are certain scaling percentages that will ensure that the patterns stay sharp and clear. 👁 See "Scaling a Style" on pages 10–11.*

Original Graphic **Wow-Plastic 01** **Wow-Plastic 02**

Wow-Plastic 03* **Wow-Plastic 04** **Wow-Plastic 05 ***

Wow-Plastic 06 **Wow-Plastic 07** **Wow-Plastic 08**

Wow-Plastic 09

Wow-Plastic 10

Wow-Plastic 11

Wow-Plastic 12

Wow-Plastic 13 *

Wow-Plastic 14 *

Wow-Plastic 15

Wow-Plastic 16

Wow-Plastic 17

Wow-Plastic 18 *

Wow-Plastic 19

Wow-Plastic 20

Polished & Textured Woods

The Layer Styles in the **Wow-Woods** set provide the look of wood — common or exotic, raw or polished, or even encased in resin. In some the wood surfaces are smooth, while in others the grain is raised.

After you've applied a **Wow-Woods** Style, you can change the drop shadow by double-clicking the icon beside the layer's name in the Layers palette, then clicking on Drop Shadow in the list of effects in the Layer Style dialog box and adjusting the shadow parameters. 👁 *See "Scaling a Style" on pages 10–11 for the relationship between Layer Styles and the Resolution setting.*

The names of all the Styles in the Wow-Woods set include the * symbol, which indicates that a surface pattern or texture is part of the Style. If you need to scale one of these Styles to fit your file, there are certain scaling percentages that will ensure that the patterns stay sharp and clear. 👁 *See "Scaling a Style" on pages 10–11.*

Original Graphic

Wow-Woods 01*

Wow-Woods 02*

Wow-Woods 03*

Wow-Woods 04*

Wow-Woods 05*

Wow-Woods 06*

Wow-Woods 07*

Wow-Woods 08*

Wow-Woods 09*

Wow-Woods 10*

Wow-Woods 11*

Wow-Woods 12*

Wow-Woods 13*

Wow-Woods 14*

Wow-Woods 15*

Wow-Woods 16*

Wow-Woods 17*

Wow-Woods 18*

Wow-Woods 19*

Wow-Woods 20*

Rock, Brick & Other Materials

The Layer Styles in the **Wow-Rocks** set were designed to endow type and graphics with the textures of everything from alien minerals (**07** is molten Kryptonite) to a variety of building materials — from bricks (**01**) to rough and smooth stone (including sandstone, **20**), and even various kinds of weathered ores (**11, 13, 16,** and **19**).

The effects shown here are the results of applying the Styles to a file with a Resolution setting of 225 pixels/inch. 👁 *See "Scaling a Style" on pages 10–11 for the relationship between Layer Styles and the Resolution setting.*

The names of all the Styles in the **Wow-Rocks set include the * symbol, which indicates that a surface pattern or texture is part of the Style. If you need to scale one of these Styles to fit your file, there are certain scaling percentages that will ensure that the patterns stay sharp and clear.* 👁 *See "Scaling a Style" on pages 10–11.*

Original Graphic

Wow-Rocks 01*

Wow-Rocks 02*

Wow-Rocks 03*

Wow-Rocks 04*

Wow-Rocks 05*

Wow-Rocks 06*

Wow-Rocks 07*

Wow-Rocks 08*

Wow-Rocks 09*

Wow-Rocks 10*

Wow-Rocks 11*

Wow-Rocks 12*

Wow-Rocks 13*

Wow-Rocks 14*

Wow-Rocks 15*

Wow-Rocks 16*

Wow-Rocks 17*

Wow-Rocks 18*

Wow-Rocks 19*

Wow-Rocks 20*

Organic Patterns

The Layer Styles in the **Wow-Organics** are seamlessly wrapping photographic patterns and textures, great for backgrounds, panels, or special fills for display text or graphics. Most of the **Wow-Organics** have shadows, bevels, or subtly embossed surface textures, so these Styles can be used to turn type or graphics into dimensional objects. But these attributes can also be turned off when you simply want a background or fill. ◉ *See the tip on page 68 for changing or removing individual effects from a Style.*

The relatively large and detailed **00–03** are designed for backgrounds.

▶ *With the Pattern Overlay section of the Layer Style dialog box open, you can drag in the main image window to shift the pattern. This is especially useful for repositioning large patterns.*

Organics 04 and **05** include stroked edges and inner shadows that make them ideal for type. Style **06** shows the brush work of coarse stucco. Styles **07**, **08**, and **17–20** are woven materials whose patterns are enhanced with texture. Organics **09–12** are papers, **13** is a corroded surface with stark outlining, **14** is cork, and **15** and **16** are bamboo variations.

Wow-Organics 00*

Wow-Organics 01*

Wow-Organics 02*

Wow-Organics 03*

Wow-Organics 04*

Wow-Organics 05*

Wow-Organics 06*

Wow-Organics 07*

Wow-Organics 08*

The names of all the **Wow-Organics Styles include the * symbol, indicating a built-in surface pattern or texture. If you need to scale one of these Styles to fit your file, there are certain scaling percentages that will ensure that the patterns stay sharp and clear. ◉ See "Scaling a Style" on pages 10–11.*

Wow-Organics 09*

Wow-Organics 10*

Wow-Organics 11*

Wow-Organics 12*

Wow-Organics 13*

Wow-Organics 14*

Wow-Organics 15*

Wow-Organics 16*

Wow-Organics 17*

Wow-Organics 18*

Wow-Organics 19*

Wow-Organics 20*

Patterns & Fabrics

The Layer Styles in the **Wow-Fabric** library are seamlessly repeating patterns. The patterns are also subtly embossed on the surface, the edges are beveled, and drop shadows have been added so that these Styles can be used to turn type or graphics into dimensional objects. But these attributes can also be turned off if what you need is simply a pattern to use as a background or fill.

▶ *To change or remove any of the individual effects in a Style you've applied, simply double-click the ƒ icon for the "styled" layer in the Layers palette, then find the specific effect in the list in the Layer Style dialog box. You can "uncheck" the effect — for example, click on the check mark to the left of "Drop Shadow," "Bevel and Emboss" or "Texture" in the list. Or click the name of the effect and change the settings to taste.*

▶ *The 21 Patterns used in the **Wow-Fabric** Styles plus 24 more Patterns can be found in the **Wow 7-Fabric Patterns** library.*

Wow-Fabric 00 *

Wow-Fabric 01 *

Wow-Fabric 02 *

Wow-Fabric 03 *

Wow-Fabric 04 *

Wow-Fabric 05 *

Wow-Fabric 06 *

Wow-Fabric 07 *

Wow-Fabric 08 *

The names of all the Styles in the **Wow-Fabric library include the * symbol, which indicates that a pattern is part of the Style. If you need to scale one of these Styles to fit your file, there are certain scaling percentages that will ensure that the patterns stay sharp and clear.* ◉ *See "Scaling a Style" on pages 10–11.*

Wow-Fabric 09 *

Wow-Fabric 10 *

Wow-Fabric 11 *

Wow-Fabric 12 *

Wow-Fabric 13 *

Wow-Fabric 14 *

Wow-Fabric 15 *

Wow-Fabric 16 *

Wow-Fabric 17 *

Wow-Fabric 18 *

Wow-Fabric 19 *

Wow-Fabric 20 *

Strokes & Fills

The Layer Styles in the **Wow-Stroke** library provide everything from a simple outline, to beveled edging with a color fill, to fill treatments that look abstract or hand-painted. Some have drop shadows to "pop" the type or graphic off the page.

▶ *To change or remove any of the individual effects in a Style you've applied, simply double-click the ⓕ icon for the "styled" layer in the Layers palette, then find the specific effect in the list in the Layer Style dialog box. Either "uncheck" the effect — for example, click on the check mark to the left of "Drop Shadow" in the list. Or click the name of the effect and change the settings.*

Styles **02, 04,** and **05** use the color of the original graphic.

Styles **03** and **18–20** can make great "comic book" headlines. Styles **09–15** provide more sophisticated colors as well as subtle interior "halos," textures and gradients.

Stroke **16's** "watercolor" fill can enhance calligraphy or rough graphics. And the "crayon rubbing" fill of **17** follows the contours of the type or graphic.

Original Graphic **Wow-Stroke 01*** **Wow-Stroke 02**

Wow-Stroke 03 **Wow-Stroke 04** **Wow-Stroke 05**

Wow-Stroke 06 **Wow-Stroke 07** **Wow-Stroke 08**

*Styles whose names include the * symbol have a built-in surface pattern or texture. If you need to scale one of these Styles to fit your file, there are certain scaling percentages that will ensure that the patterns stay sharp and clear. ◉ *See "Scaling a Style" on pages 10–11.*

Wow-Stroke 09

Wow-Stroke 10

Wow-Stroke 11

Wow-Stroke 12*

Wow-Stroke 13*

Wow-Stroke 14*

Wow-Stroke 15

Wow-Stroke 16*

Wow-Stroke 17*

Wow-Stroke 18

Wow-Stroke 19

Wow-Stroke 20

Shadows, Halos & Embossing

Many of the **Wow-Halo** Styles are "positive and negative" pairs. So you'll find, side by side on these pages, two versions of the same general Style — one dark and one light, or one raised above the surface and one impressed into it. Shown here are the results of applying the Styles to a file with a Resolution setting of 225 pixels/inch.

The simple halos (**03** and **04**) and the rainbow Styles (**15** and **16**) keep the original fill color (here 50% gray). (The rainbows work well against "middle-tone" backgrounds rather than pure black or white.) The "noisy" halos (**05** and **06** as well as **13** and **14**) replace the original color with black and white. In all the other **Wow-Halos** the original type or graphic disappears, and the shape is defined by the halo, shadow, or embossed edge.

Styles **09** and **10** are sharp-edged and rounded versions of carved effects. **Halo 11** is a sharply embossed stamp effect, and **Halo 12** is a subtle raised emboss treatment.

Original Graphic   Wow-Halo 01   Wow-Halo 02

Wow-Halo 03   Wow-Halo 04   Wow-Halo 05

Wow-Halo 06   Wow-Halo 07   Wow-Halo 08

Wow-Halo 09

Wow-Halo 10

Wow-Halo 11

Wow-Halo 12

Wow-Halo 13

Wow-Halo 14

Wow-Halo 15

Wow-Halo 16

Wow-Halo 17

Wow-Halo 18

Wow-Halo 19

Wow-Halo 20

Glows & Neons

Most of the **Wow-Glows** work best when you apply them to type or graphics used against dark or middle-tone backgrounds that contrast with their glowing light. Shown here are the results of applying the Styles to a file with a Resolution setting of 225 pixels/inch.

The multicolor glows (**18–20**) keep the original fill color of the graphic, while all the other **Wow-Glows** Styles replace the original color with the colors shown here.

Styles **03–05** are the "off" versions of the "lit" neons created by **06–08**. In these and other neons (**10–12** and **17**), the fill of the type or graphic is eliminated, and the edges are traced with "neon tubes."

You can use **Glows 09** to turn type and graphics into a glowing "plasma field," or **13–16** to make them "burn."

Original Graphic

Wow-Glows 01

Wow-Glows 02

Wow-Glows 03

Wow-Glows 04

Wow-Glows 05

Wow-Glows 06

Wow-Glows 07

Wow-Glows 08

Wow-Glows 09

Wow-Glows 10

Wow-Glows 11

Wow-Glows 12

Wow-Glows 13

Wow-Glows 14

Wow-Glows 15

Wow-Glows 16

Wow-Glows 17

Wow-Glows 18

Wow-Glows 19

Wow-Glows 20

Button Rollover Styles

The **Wow-Button** Styles were designed to look good when applied to small on-screen navigational elements created at 72 pixels/inch. As shown in the palette below, the **Wow 7–20 Button Styles.asl** file is made up of sets of three individual Styles designed especially for the **Normal, Over,** and **Down** states of buttons, as well as a fourth **All Three** Style. The **Normal, Over,** and **Down** Styles (shown here left-to-right) don't have built-in rollover properties. You can use them individually in Photoshop or ImageReady. But the **All Three** Styles include the JavaScript for interactivity — in ImageReady if you apply an **All Three** Style to a button graphic, the button will change in response to what the user does with the cursor. ◉ *See "Working with Styles in ImageReady" on page 17 for more about Rollover Styles.*

The top three rows of Styles in each column (**01–03, 11–13, 21–23, 31–33,** and **41–43**) are color variations of five basic Styles.

Most of the **Wow-Button** Styles replace the original color. But Style **09** retains the underlying color of the graphic or photo.

*Styles whose names include the * symbol have a built-in surface pattern or texture. If you need to scale one of these Styles to fit your file, there are certain scaling percentages that will ensure that the patterns stay sharp and clear. ◉ See "Scaling a Style" on pages 10–11 for help.*

4 Other Wow! Presets

👁 *For extensive step-by-step techniques for painting, cropping, retouching images, and making and using Patterns and Gradients, see the latest version of* The Photoshop Wow! Book *(Dayton & Davis, Peachpit Press).*

The world of **One-Click Wow!** holds a lot more than just Styles — from painting to retouching to eye-popping special effects, all done with Presets. If you followed the instructions in steps 1 and 2 on page 3, you'll find these **Wow 7 Presets** in your Photoshop menus:

- In the pop-out menu of the **Tool Presets** palette are the **Wow 7-Art History Brushes**, **Wow 7-Pattern Stamp Brushes**, and **Wow 7-Art Media Brushes**, with more than 60 tools for simulating traditional artists' media — including Pastel, Chalk, Oil, Watercolor, Sponge, Stipple, and Dry Brush. See pages 79–81 and 84–85 for instructions and samples of these Presets for the Pattern Stamp, Art History Brush, and Brush. Also find a gallery of examples on pages 82–83.

- Also available in the **Tool Presets** palette's menu are the **Wow 7-Image Fix Brushes**, Presets for the Brush tool, for correcting color and tone, removing red-eye, whitening eyes and teeth, and neutralizing redness on the skin. See "Using the Wow! Image Fix Brushes" on page 86 for pointers.

- Finally, **Wow 7 Presets** for the Rectangular **Marquee Tool** and **Crop Tool** will help you make selections at many popular sizes and crop images to those dimensions.

- The **Wow 7-Actions** — for production shortcuts; enhancing paintings, photos, and graphics; and fixing images — are covered on pages 87–89.

- There are **Wow 7-Patterns** for printed Fabric, Marble, Media substrates, Miscellaneous Surfaces, Noise (which can be used for artistic treatments or to simulate film grain), and Organic materials such as wood and woven fibers. The **Wow 7-Patterns** will be available from the pop-out menu anywhere the Patterns palette occurs; for instance, in the Fill dialog box (opened by choosing Edit > Fill), in the Pattern Fill dialog (opened when you click the "Create new fill or adjustment layer" button at the bottom of the Layers palette), in the Options bar for the Pattern Stamp or Paint Bucket tool, or in certain Style components that use Patterns (such as the Pattern Overlay, the Stroke, and the Texture "subeffect" of Bevel And Emboss).

- Using the **Wow 7-Gradients** is described on page 90.

▶ *The names of the Wow 7-Crop Tool Presets tell you the specific dimensions and Resolution setting that will be produced when you crop. The image will be resampled when you make the Crop. This may "soften" the image — in some cases so much that you may want to Undo and choose a Crop with a larger area or a lower Resolution setting. In other cases you can sharpen the image by using the Unsharp Mask filter.* 👁 *See "Sharpening" on page 21 for tips.*

HOW TO PAINT WITH THE WOW! PAINT & CLONE PRESETS

Turn an existing photo into a painting with the Wow 7-Pattern Stamp or Wow 7-Art History Brushes. Or start with a blank canvas and paint from scratch with the Wow 7-Art Media Brushes. All three types of brushes have matching brush tips, so you can switch back and forth seamlessly between the three painting methods.

There are two kinds of Wow cloning brushes — the Pattern Stamp (**PS**) Presets that pull color from a source image as you paint stroke-by-stroke, and the Art History Brush (**AH**) Presets that automatically follow the color and contrast in the source image to create brush strokes. With either of these kinds of tools, you can turn a photo into a painting in five easy-to-understand steps. This process is described first for the **Wow-Pattern Stamp Brushes**, and then (on page 81) for the **Wow-Art History Brushes**. Before you start, be sure the **Wow-Tools**, **Wow-Photoshop Actions**, and **Wow-Styles** folders have been installed. 👁 *See step 1 on page 3 if you need instructions.*

1 Preparing the photo. Choose the photo you want to turn into a painting. Save a copy of the file (**File > Save As** under a new name) so you'll have the original if you need to go back to it.

*This landscape was chosen as the basis for the cloned painting to be made with **Wow-PS Watercolor** brushes.*

Then make any changes that you like to the copy. For instance:

- Exaggerate its color and contrast if you like, until you have the colors you want in your painting.

After the image was cropped, the contrast was increased and the color exaggerated using Levels and Hue/Saturation adjustments.

- If you want your painting to have an "unfinished edges" look, make a selection of the edges and fill it with white. 👁 *See pages 82–83 for several examples of paintings done this way.*

2 Loading "paint" into the brush. To make the image the source for painting with the **Wow-PS** Presets, define it as a Pattern by choosing Edit > Define Pattern; everything that's visible will become a Pattern tile.

In the Pattern Name dialog box, type in a name and click "OK."

Now make this new Pattern the cloning source for the painting: **Choose the Pattern Stamp** from the Tools palette and **choose your new pattern** from the pop-out menu of Pattern swatches in the tool's Options bar.

Choosing the Pattern Stamp; it shares a space with the Clone Stamp.

Clicking the little arrow to the right of the Pattern swatch in the Options bar opens the palette of samples so you can choose the Pattern you defined.

3 Making a "canvas"/surface layer. This step will add a surface layer above your image to make a foundation for your painting and to serve as a visual barrier between your original image and the painting layer so you'll be able to see your brush strokes clearly as your painting develops. One way to do this is to click the "Create new fill or adjustment layer" button at the bottom of the Layers palette, choose Solid Color, and pick white. When the new layer appears in the Layers palette, reduce its Opacity.

With a Color Fill layer added and its Opacity reduced, you can see your photo.

► *Using a Wacom pressure-sensitive tablet and stylus with the **Wow-Paint&Clone Tool Presets** gives you better control than using a mouse.* 👁 *See the tip on page 81 to compare. But even if you use a mouse, you can vary the size of the brush tip by keeping your fingers on the bracket keys and toggling the brush size up and down.*

*Tapping the **[** key makes a brush tip smaller; tapping **]** enlarges the brush tip.*

► *Be sure to take advantage of the three to five sizes of each kind of brush provided in the **Wow-Pattern Stamp** brushes, **Wow-Art History** brushes, and **Wow-Art Media** brushes. Even though you can change brush tip size by using the bracket keys, you'll get much better-looking brush strokes if you start with the brush that's closest to the size you want and then enlarge or reduce it slightly with the bracket keys.*

4 Preparing a paint layer and painting. Click the "Create a new layer" button at the bottom of the Layers palette to add a transparent layer for painting. Then, with the Pattern Stamp still chosen (from step 2), in the Tool Presets palette choose one of the **Wow-PS** Presets; the **Wow-PS Watercolor** brushes were used for this example.

*Each type of **Wow-PS** brush is provided in at least three sizes so you can find the one that best matches the level of detail you want at any point in your painting.*

Now paint, keeping these pointers in mind:

• In general start with a larger brush and move to smaller ones as you add finer details.

• Try to paint each differently colored area separately.

• Don't "scrub" over the image, but instead make brush strokes that follow the color and shape contours.

From time to time, increase the Opacity of the Color Fill layer to hide the original image so you can see how the painting is developing.

Viewing the painting in progress, with the Opacity of the Color Fill layer at 75% (left) and at 100% (right)

After you've used cloning brushes to create the painting, you may want to use a matching (non-cloning) **Wow 7-Art Media Brushes** Preset with the Brush tool and a very small brush tip, for full control as you paint the finest details. Choose colors for the Brush by Alt/Option-clicking in your paint layer.

5 Enhancing the painting. When the painting is complete, you may want to try one of these techniques to add to it:

• Increase the density of the color by making a copy of the paint layer (target the paint layer by clicking its name in the Layers palette, and then press Ctrl/⌘-J to copy it). This extra layer will build up any strokes that are partially transparent, to intensify the color.

*The **Wow-PS Watercolor** painting with all brush strokes completed (left) and after building up the color by duplicating the paint layer (right)*

If you like the result, with the duplicate (top) paint layer active, press Ctrl/⌘-E to merge the two paint layers together.

• Target the paint layer in the Layers palette and run one of the **Wow-Paint Edge Enhance** Actions by clicking on it in the Actions palette.

*Before (left) and after running the **Wow-Paint Edge Enhance-Subtle** Action*

▶ **The Wow-Art Media Brushes** *Presets were designed for creating paintings of your own, without cloning a photo. (The names of these Presets start with "BT," which stands for "Brush Tool," which is the tool you choose in the Tools palette in order to work with these Presets chosen from the Tool Presets palette.) Of course, these brushes can also be used for adding the finishing touches to a cloned painting as well. Strokes made with the **Wow-BT** brushes are shown below.*

Wow-BT Chalk

Wow-BT Dry Brush

Wow-BT Oil

Wow-BT Pastel

Wow-BT Sponge

Wow-BT Stipple

Wow-BT Watercolor

*Strokes painted with the seven kinds of **Wow-Art Media Brushes**. In each case the top stroke was produced with the mouse and the bottom one with a Wacom Intuos tablet.*

*The **Wow-Paint Edge Enhance Actions** work by filtering a copy of the paint layer and using Blend Modes to combine it with what's below.*

- Painting with the **Wow Presets** creates canvas or paper texture as well as brush strokes. You can make these more apparent by applying one of the **Wow-Texture Styles** to the paint layers. See examples of the **Wow-Textures** on pages 44–45.

*Applying **Wow-Texture 01** to the painting layer*

To paint with the **Wow-Art History Brush Presets**, the five-step process goes like this:

1 Preparing the photo. Use the same procedure described in step 1 on page 79.

2 Loading "paint" into the brush. To define your photo as the source, open the History palette (**choose Window > History**) and **choose New Snapshot** from the menu that pops out from the upper right corner of the palette; choose **Merged Layers** from the pop-out menu in the New Snapshot dialog box.

*Making a "Merged Layers" Snapshot of your enhanced photo, to act as a source for the **Wow-AH** brushes.*

In the History palette, **click in the column to the left of the Snapshot** you just made; this

sets it as the source for painting. Then **choose the Art History Brush from the Tools palette,** and **choose one of the Wow-AH brushes from the Tool Presets palette.**

Defining your Merged Snapshot as the source

The Art History Brush shares a spot with the History Brush.

3 Making a "canvas" layer. Use the same procedure described in step 3 on page 79.

4 Preparing a paint layer, and painting. Add an empty layer as described in step 4 on page 79. Then with the Art History Brush and **Wow-AH brush** chosen in step 2, **click on an area of contrast** to generate a series of brush strokes. Start with larger brushes and proceed to smaller ones until the canvas is filled with painted strokes.

*The painting was started with the **Wow-AH Oil-Large** Tool Preset (left) and then details were added with the **Medium** and **Small** versions (right).*

5 Enhancing the painting. To improve color or texture, use any of the techniques described in step 5 starting on page 80.

*The oil painting after duplicating the paint layer, running the **Wow-Paint Edge Enhance-Subtle** Action, and applying the **Wow-Texture 01** Layer Style*

PAINTING GALLERY

These "cloned" paintings were made using some of the **Wow-Pattern Stamp (PS)** and **Wow-Art History (AH)** presets shown on pages 84–85 and the methods described on pages 79–81. They were done at various sizes and Resolution settings and reduced to fit this layout.*

1 The strokes of the **PS Dry Brush** tools were enhanced with the **Texture 03** Style. **2 PS Chalk** with **Texture 07** creates the look of dry chalk on rough board. **3** This stylized illustration was converted to a painting using **PS Dry Brush** with **Texture 03**. **4 PS Watercolor** with **Texture 01** and **5 AH Oil** with **Texture 02** create two very different results from the same photo. **6 PS Watercolor**, with its Wet Edges and Airbrush settings, was used with **Texture 09** for a wet-into-wet effect. **7 AH Sponge** and **Texture 10** simulate paint dabbed onto stucco. **8 PS Watercolor** (with **Texture 01**) was used with smaller brush tips than in 4. **9** The automated strokes of the **AH Watercolor** tools, here with **Texture 01**, create a soft "wash" effect. **10** The pastel work was automated with **AH Chalk**, again with **Texture 01**. **11** Precise brush work for fine detail was created by using **PS Watercolor** and **Texture 01**.

*After they were painted, these images were enhanced by running the **Wow-Darken Edges** Action (shown on page 88) on the "paint" layer. It duplicates the layer, runs the Photocopy filter, and then sets the mode of the filtered layer to Color Burn.

Pattern Stamp & Art History Presets

On these two pages are paintings made from the photo below, using the **Wow 7-Pattern Stamp Brushes** and **Wow 7-Art History Brushes**. These paintings were produced using a Wacom tablet and the five-step method outlined in "How To Paint with the Wow! Paint & Clone Presets" on pages 79-81. The label under each picture tells which Tool Preset and Texture Style (from pages 44–45) were used.

With the **Wow 7-Pattern Stamp (PS) Brushes**, you hand-paint each cloning stroke. The **Wow 7-Art History (AH) Brushes** are set up to apply strokes that automatically follow the contrast and color features of the source image. They clone much faster than the PS tools, but the automation means you have less creative control.

▶ *Here are some tips for using Wow-PS Watercolor Presets:*

• *To imitate a wash, use one continuous stroke rather than starting and stopping.*

• *Don't let colors touch or the details will blur.*

• *To add density to your watercolor, duplicate the painted layer (Ctrl/⌘-J) so the partially transparent colors build, and then adjust the Opacity of this top layer to taste.*

ORIGINAL PHOTO & PAINTINGS: JACK H. DAVIS

Wow-PS Watercolor + Texture 01

Wow-PS Oil + Texture 03

Wow-PS Dry Brush + Texture 02

Wow-PS Chalk + Texture 07

Wow-AH Watercolor + Texture 01

Wow-AH Oil + Texture 02

Wow-AH Pastel + Texture 01

Wow-AH Chalk + Texture 07

Wow-AH Stipple + Texture 10

Wow-AH Sponge + Texture 09

USING THE WOW! IMAGE FIX BRUSHES

Use these "fix-it" tools to tackle common problems.

▶ *Photoshop 7's new Healing Brush can be really useful for hiding blemishes and smoothing wrinkles. Here's an approach that does both, with a degree of subtlety that doesn't make skin look unnaturally smooth:*

1 *Duplicate the original photo to a new layer (Ctrl/⌘-J) and use the Healing Brush on anything you want to remove completely, such as **blemishes**, as described in the Photoshop 7 User Guide.*

2 *Duplicate this "healed" layer (Ctrl/⌘-J), then use the Healing Brush again, this time to remove the **wrinkles**. Then adjust the Opacity of this "wrinkles" layer to let some of the original "character lines" show through.*

The process of improving a photo should start with overall tone and color adjustments and then proceed to retouching tasks. Here are some pointers for success:

1 Duplicate your image file (choose File > Save As and save under a new name). In case you make a mistake in your retouching, you'll have your original to go back to.

2 Then make any necessary corrections to overall tone and color. You can try one of the **Wow-Image Fix Actions** to correct overall problems. If the result isn't quite what you want, in the Layers palette drag the Adjustment layer made by the Action to the trash can button at the bottom of the palette, then try a different **Wow-Image Fix Action**. 👁 *See "Using the Wow! Actions" on page 87 for directions.* Other subtle "quick fixes" you can try are **Wow-Darkroom Styles 11–15**; these are variations of **Wow-Darkroom 03**, which darkens the edges and lightens the center.

*Try **Wow-Darkroom Styles 11–15** to brighten an image. Step 4 on page 4 tells how to apply a Style.*

3 Once you've made the overall corrections, you can go to work with the **Wow-Image Fix** brushes. With the **Wow-Tools** folder stored inside your Photoshop 7 Tools folder (as described in step 1 on page 3), choose the Brush tool from Photoshop's Tools palette, then open the Tool Presets palette (**Window > Tool Presets**). Choose **Wow-Image Fix Brushes** from the palette's pop-out list, and use them as shown at the right.

To even the lighting in an image, in the Tool Presets palette, choose a **Wow-Dodge&Burn** tool from the Tool Presets palette, and paint with it, switching between black (to darken) and white (to lighten). Aim for subtle changes.

*Before (left) and after lightening with the **Wow-Dodge&Burn-Subtle** Preset, using white paint, a large soft brush tip, and low Opacity.*

To get rid of "red-eye," first use the **Wow-Red Eye-Neutralize** brush at an appropriate size to carefully paint away the red in the pupil (and the iris if necessary). If you do have to remove red from the iris, restore color with one of the three **Wow-Red Eye-Replace** brushes. And if the pupil needs darkening, use the **Wow-Red Eye-Darken** brush.

*To correct red-eye, neutralize the red and restore color to the iris if necessary (center), and then darken the pupil if needed (right). You can use the bracket keys to change brush size — **[** to go smaller, **]** to enlarge.*

To whiten teeth or eyes, dab with an appropriate-size **Wow-White Teeth-Neutralize** brush to get rid of stains. (Stay away from lips and gums.) Then use the **Wow-White Teeth-Brighten** brush to lighten.

*Rather than aiming for a "Hollywood" smile, use the **Wow-White Teeth** brushes to neutralize specific stained areas (center), then whiten them (right).*

To take the "heat" out of red patches on the face but still leave some of the natural blush, use the **Wow-Red Skin-Neutralize** brush.

*If the built-in color of the **Wow-Red Skin-Neutralize** brush isn't right for your image, hold down the Alt/Option key and click in the image to sample skin color.*

USING THE WOW! ACTIONS

These "try 'em, you'll like 'em" Wow! Actions meet everyday Photoshop challenges and create some spectacular effects.

▶ *Before you run any Action (Wow or not), make yourself a "safety net" by duplicating the file (choose Image > Duplicate).* **If you run the Action and don't like the result, close the "actioned" duplicate without saving it, go back to your original file, duplicate it again, and try a different Action. You can also use this safety net if a "Stop" message box appears as part of the Action and you decide you don't want to continue.**

▶ **With your Actions palette in list mode:**

- *Ctrl/⌘-clicking* **on an Action's name** *plays the Action.*
- **Double-clicking to the right of the name** *allows you to assign an F-key to the Action.*

There are five sets of Wow-Actions — "mini-programs" you can run in Photoshop for image fixing, dimensional effects for graphics, photo enhancements, enhancements for paintings, and production shortcuts.

1 Setting up the Actions palette. Once you've copied the **Wow Actions** into the Photoshop Actions folder as described in step 1 on page 3, open the Actions palette (**choose Window > Actions**). By default the palette appears in List Mode, but you can toggle it to a compact and colorful set of buttons by choosing **Button Mode** from the menu that pops out from the palette's upper right corner. Each **Wow 7-Actions** set that you choose from the bottom of that menu will be added to the palette.

2 Preparing the file. Open the file you want to run a Wow Action on. Duplicate the file (choose Image > Duplicate and click "OK") so you'll have a "pre-Action" backup in case you don't like the result of the Action. In your duplicate file, make sure the image you want to start with is what's showing on-screen. That is, all the layers, masks, and Styles that make up the image must be visible. Also, target the layer you want the Action to work on (**click on the layer's name** in the Layers palette).

3 "Playing" the Action. In the Actions palette, click the button for the Action you want to run. Basically, that's it — the Action runs!

Some of the Wow Actions start by making a duplicate file from whatever is visible in your image file. The Action then runs on that copy.

But if a "Stop" message box appears (it has a "Stop" button and often a "Continue" button also), be sure to read what it says and follow its instructions — it may tell you to make a selection, customize a setting, or adjust something to taste. If you don't do it, the Action won't work correctly.

Click the button to start the Action (above). It's important to read and carry out the directions in any "Stop" message. Then click the button again (it will be red, so you can find it) to continue.

Briefly, here are some examples of what the **Wow Actions** do:

Wow 7-Image Fix Actions. Among these is **Wow 7-Dust & Scratches Layer**, which helps you remove those tiny, annoying specks; it's faster than using Photoshop's Healing Brush, and you do the work on a separate layer, so you can't accidentally make your original worse. **Wow 7-Auto Levels Sampler** adds several Levels Adjustment layers for correcting common tone and color problems; after running the Action you can view the effect of each Adjustment layer and choose which works best. ◉ *See page 89 for more.*

Wow 7-Graphics Enhance Actions. These routines turn your active graphics or type layer into materials with characteristics like refraction or flame, which are too complex to achieve with a single Style.

Wow 7-Paint Enhance Actions. Try these after using the Wow painting and cloning Presets, to emphasize brush strokes or pooled paint.

Wow 7-Photo Enhance Actions. Try any of these 21 enhancements, such as watercolor, mezzotint, and framing, and see what happens.

Wow 7-Production Actions. These are shortcuts (especially in Button Mode) for everyday operations, like rotating a digital photo 90°.

WOW! ACTIONS

Shown on these two pages are just some of the effects you can accomplish by running the **Wow-Actions,** which are multi-step automated "macros" that come in five sets. The examples on this page are from the **Wow-Graphics Enhance** Actions, and the examples on page 89 are from the **Wow-Photo Enhance** set, with the exception of one from the **Wow-Image Fix** set. (The starting graphic and photo are provided in the **Wow-Actions Testers** folder on the CD-ROM so you can experiment by running the **Wow-Actions** on them if you like.)

The **Wow Actions** are quick, "try 'em, you'll like 'em" options. Some of them are as "instant" as Layer Styles. Others require that you interact with the Action as it runs. Follow the steps on page 87 to add these Actions to Photoshop's Actions palette, then to make a duplicate of your file, and finally to play an Action. **If a "Stop" message box appears, read and follow its instructions carefully — the Action needs your undivided attention at this point in order to get the right results.**

Wow-Brushed Steel

Wow-Fire

Wow-Oiled Steel

Wow-Crystal

Wow-Gold

Wow-Chrome

*The **Wow Chrome and Crystal Actions** use your background photo for the reflection.*

Wow-Silver

Wow-Distressed

Wow-Brushed Metal

Wow-Dodge & Burn Layer
*From the **Wow-Image Fix** set;*
before (right) and after (left)

Wow-Color Background

Wow-Background Blur

Wow-Channel Mix-Pastels

Wow-Filtered Watercolor

Wow-Filtered Water+Line

Wow-Soft Focus-Lighten

Wow-Soft Focus-Overlay

Wow-Mezzotint-Gray

Wow-Linework Alone

Wow-Filtered Frame-Soft

Wow-Filtered Frame-Wood

GRADIENT FILLS

The **Wow-Gradients** can be useful for filling type or graphics, or even for creating a background element. Three of the "rainbow" gradients (**04–06**) create transparent top and bottom edges.

The **Wow-Gradients** can be applied to fill an entire new layer by clicking the "Create new fill or adjustment layer" button at the bottom of the Layers palette and choosing Gradient Fill from the pop-up list. Or you can fill a selected area by using the Gradient tool or the Edit > Fill command, choosing "Gradient" in the Fill dialog box. **Wow-Gradients 27–31** were designed to be applied as Radial gradients inside a round selection, to create the highlighting and shadows needed for the dimensionality of a balloon, for instance.

A **Wow-Gradient** can also be built into a Style as an overlay by opening the Layer Style dialog box and clicking on "Gradient Overlay" in the list at the left side of the box, then choosing a Gradient, Style, and Angle. You can also use a Gradient as the Stroke component of a Style.